SUPER
BOARDS

Praise for *Super Boards* and *The Board Game*

"Bill Mott has done it again. Building on his wonderful morality tale, *The Board Game*, Bill's new book, *Super Boards*, provides an insightful blueprint for building and sustaining transformational governing boards. Bill's counsel provides both philosophical and practical advice for organizations and the servant-leaders who possess the power to truly change organizations for the better."

—**Scott Wilson**
Headmaster, Baylor School, Chattanooga, Tennessee

"Boards play a pivotal role in shaping the vision and direction for any school or nonprofit organization. Dr. Bill Mott shares his expertise and experience in his second book, *Super Boards*, as a comprehensive leadership guide. This book should be required reading for all leaders and board members as they work together to become a 'super' leadership group in order to maximize the impact of the school or nonprofit organization in the local community or across the globe."

—**Rick Newberry, Ph.D.**
President, Enrollment Catalyst

"*Super Boards* is super-charged with applicable case stories, insightful checklists, and illuminating questions that accompany each chapter and delve into the complexities we rarely read about but often grapple with in board leadership. Every nonprofit executive and board member aspiring to perform at the highest level of governance should apply Bill Mott's thoughtful views so they can make the best decisions on behalf of the organizations they care so much about."

—**Denise McMahan**
Founder, CausePlanet

"If you're a board member or an executive director looking to develop a 'board of trust'—a group who act and perform their responsibilities as a cohesive unit rather than the standard 'board of trustees,' *Super Boards* is the book you need to put at the top of your reading list. By applying the lessons shared in this book, you will be well on your way to creating a Super Board."

—Natasha Golinsky
Founder, Next Level Nonprofits

"In today's hypercompetitive nonprofit world, an exceptional board of directors is critically important for every nonprofit of whatever size or purpose. Bill Mott's new book, *Super Boards*, provides a description of what an exceptional board looks and functions like. It is a road map for how boards can assess themselves and develop a plan to achieve their desired exceptionalism. Bill shows us a clear-cut way to be the best we can be. Thank you Bill!"

—Howard J. Kittell
President and CEO, The Hermitage, Home of President Andrew Jackson

"The work of school and other nonprofit leadership demands a clear understanding of the role of effective governance in allowing the organization to reach its potential. The case studies contained in *Super Boards* are especially helpful in illustrating the challenges and opportunities that we as school and other nonprofit leaders face. These case studies will enable us to engage with our trustees and others in the school community in meaningful dialogue about best practices. These narratives contain illustrative examples and cautionary tales that ring true."

—Dr. John W. Griffith
Head of School, Ranney School

"*Super Boards* offers a step-by-step guide in building a governing board and sustaining its success through aligning people, positions, and plans with purpose. Bill has included some very thoughtful points that are often missed by many when building, serving on, or working with a board. This practical how-to book outlines positive actions for helping a board of trustees, and those who influence its actions, achieve the vital coming together as one voice."

—SusanBeth Stanford Purifico
Director of Program Design & Development, We R 3C, Inc.

"For nonprofit leaders who are interested in recruiting and developing the most effective boards for their organizations comes a blueprint for success in *Super Boards*, written by a nonprofit leader who has sat on both sides of the table in the board room. *Super Boards* includes hands-on ways to strengthen the crucial relationship between the CEO and board chair and points out pitfalls to avoid in order to be a successful nonprofit organization. Any nonprofit or school leader and board chair who hopes to develop a strong leadership team would benefit by using Dr. Mott's case studies with their boards as a basis for discussion."

—Ian Craig
Head of School, Harding Academy

"Bill Mott has crafted a very readable and insightful book depicting common board dilemmas, which provides a great opportunity for engaging board members in a study of board quality and best practice. Placing these lessons within case study form rather than from the typical didactic lecture method invites discussion and more in-depth learning."

—Steve Hammond
Principal, Head of School, St. Patrick Catholic School

"He's done it again! As he did with *The Board Game*, William Mott has written a book that inspires organizations to take an honest look at the status quo and spurs an open dialogue about how transformational leadership can revitalize nonprofits. *Super Boards* urges us to think differently, to be open about governance, and to be deliberate in developing the cultures of our organizations. With concrete language and examples that resonate throughout the nonprofit community, William Mott provides us with an outline of steps that are essential in establishing an effective board culture from which organizations can flourish. I consider it a must-read for all board members and nonprofit executives."

—Kasey Anderson
Executive Director, Nashville Academy of Medicine

"Nonprofit organizations cannot excel without a highly functional board. Although many manage to muddle through fulfilling their mission without focused leadership, it takes a SUPER BOARD to accomplish extraordinary levels of effectiveness. *Super Boards* provides the standard to which all nonprofit boards should aspire. Bill's tenets of inspired governance will transform your organization into a SUPER NONPROFIT!"

—**Scott Parrish**
General Manager, Monteagle Sunday School Assembly

"*Super Boards* is super right on the spot. Bill Mott delivers again on what it means to develop an effective board. If you have not served on or tried to develop an effective board of directors, this book is for you. Save yourself the time and grief of not doing it right, because Dr. Mott has seen and done it all when it comes to boards. This book is an effective and precise set of rails to run your board on. With the use of case studies, Dr. Mott lays out a complete plan from recruiting to training to motivating and leading with a policy-driven board. Board members who oversee and fulfill their responsibilities as an effective board are brought to light in this collection of real-life case studies. Board governance is not easy, but *Super Boards* lays the groundwork so you can escape the pitfalls that many boards and their executives go through. Read this book! It will save the day!"

—**Hugh Harris**
Headmaster, Franklin Christian Academy

"Oh, to have had this book earlier in my nonprofit experience! Dr. Bill Mott helps us realize the importance of 'process' as well as caring about others. He is not afraid to bring out the struggles we may face; however, he takes us a step further by offering solutions, assistance, and a road map—for a continuing journey, traveling smoothly with others to reach all sorts of valuable goals along the way. *Super Boards* is a book that will be quoted often—especially in the board room where 'the value and significance of working together' is essential."

—**Brenda Hauk**
Executive Director, BrightStone

"I realize there are many other books about nonprofit governing boards, but *Super Boards* really gets to the heart of issues. Dr. Mott is very insightful and offers excellent advice."

—**Rick Wimberly**
Board Member, Williamson County Education Foundation

"In *Super Boards*, Bill Mott provides nonprofit leaders a true road map for creating a culture of excellence. He masterfully deconstructs the vital role of a strong board in the success of a nonprofit organization, examining and contrasting each element and teaching the reader to do the same. His insightful case studies are right on the mark—providing a window into the challenges faced by staff and board members alike in maintaining the delicate balance of autonomy versus accountability. Bill's sharp wit and conversational tone make for a thoroughly delightful read—one I highly recommend for any nonprofit executive or board member."

—**Rob Ivy**
Chief Financial Officer, YMCA of Middle Tennessee

"I loved *Super Boards*! Dr. Mott's second book is a gift to nonprofit leaders, both experienced and new. It is written with simplicity and clarity, providing case studies that 'bring it home' to anyone who has ever served on a nonprofit board. An easy and enjoyable read, most importantly it concisely identifies the critical challenges of nonprofit boards. Written by a person who has had real-life experiences working with boards for more than 30 years, this is absolutely a must-read and a book every board should have available to its members and future recruits."

—**Brenda S. Speer**
Chair, Capital Campaign
Giles County Public Library, Pulaski, Tennessee

"Dr. Mott's experiences as a successful board member and a successful leader are apparent throughout *Super Boards*. If your organization is ready to transform—to stop just filling board seats and to start building a 'board of trust' that is ready, willing, and able to produce dynamic and effective results, then look no further than this book. Dr. Mott provides you with the case studies, practical tools, and reflective exercises necessary to change the way your board sees itself and its role in the world."

—**Kelley Pujol, Ed.D.**
Coordinator of Cohort Programs & Evening Services
Columbia State Community College

"Bill Mott's latest book, *Super Boards*, clearly establishes him as one of the most skillful, trusted nonprofit governance advisory sources today. *Super Boards* provides a comprehensive checklist of critical considerations for any nonprofit executive director or board chair to help ensure the successful operation of their organization's 'board of trust.' Bill's case studies are extensive, thought-provoking, and at times painfully reminiscent of some of my own board experiences. The information included in the book's appendices (sample agendas, checklists, key issues) *alone* is worth the investment as a non-profit governance reference source! I highly recommend *Super Boards* to anyone wanting to strengthen their nonprofit leadership skills!"

—**Dan Haile**
Managing Principal, Haile Coaching & Leadership

"*Super Boards* offers concise, fresh, and practical guidance for anyone invested in school or nonprofit leadership. Bill Mott's diverse experience at all levels of governance enables him to write with great empathy and hard-won practical wisdom. The result is a 'Swiss Army knife' of a book—an accessible and multipurpose resource that is as useful for seasoned CEOs as it is for first-time board members. I highly recommend it!"

—**Morgan Wills, MD**
President & CEO, Siloam Family Health Center

"Nonprofit organizations rise and fall based on the capacity of the board's leadership. In this book Bill Mott has captured compelling strategies for board growth that can have profound impact on mission and effectiveness. This is a leadership role that requires continuous learning in the best practices of good governance, and *Super Boards* should be included in the library of every board member."

—**Scott Barron**
Founder, School Growth

SUPER
BOARDS

*How Inspired Governance
Transforms Your Organization*

WILLIAM R. MOTT, PH.D.

Editorial—KLOPublishing.com
Typesetting—theDESKonline.com
Cover design—DualIdentityDesign.com
Professional publishing services provided
   by Dan Wright Publisher Services LLC

The book is dedicated to my wife, Courtney,
and our children,
Courtney Leigh, Robert, and his wife, Lauren.

It is also dedicated to my late father,
Charles R. Mott, Jr.

And brother, Michael I. Mott, Sr.

CONTENTS

Chapter One • 5
VOLUNTEER BOARDS—VOLUNTEER LEADERS
Volunteer boards are an essential part of every nonprofit organization. They are required by both state and federal law and therefore play a central role in the organization's ability to achieve its mission and vision.

Chapter Two • 9
RECRUITING INSPIRED BOARD MEMBERS
Recruiting and maintaining the most inspired board members possible is the joint responsibility of the board's Committee on Trustees, all board members, and the organization's staff.

CASE STUDY #1: *"We have an opening on our board..."*   15
Recruiting board members is an intentional and thoughtful undertaking that takes place in an environment conducive to engaging in a discussion that represents the serious nature of what is at stake. Perhaps someone's front yard where you are admiring their flowers is not exactly the venue that will yield the best possible candidates.

Chapter Three • 17
TRAINING AND ORIENTATION FOR BOARD MEMBERS
In many nonprofit organizations several board members typically, or often, join the board at a specified time of the year, thus creating a "class" of new board members who begin and potentially are re-elected or rotate off at the same time.

CASE STUDY #2: *Shifting Expectations*   25
The transition that leads from one board chair to the next can result in unintended consequences. Does the new board chair have a different set of expectations than the previous chair? How do these shifting expectations impact the CEO? This is defining moment for an organization wishing to reach a new level of maturity.

Chapter Fourteen • 133
THE ROLE OF THE EXECUTIVE DIRECTOR (CEO)
The Executive Director, or CEO, of the organization has a complex job with many moving parts. It is a position of enormous responsibility and filled with challenges, opportunities, great joy, and much frustration.

CASE STUDY #11: *Changing Course in Midstream*   *139*
The president and vice president for business are ambushed at a board retreat when a trustee and former college president asks a question that creates a enormous division between the college's leadership and the trustees. Institutional memory plays a key role in understanding past policies and current circumstances. Candor and trust take a back seat in this story regarding accounts receivable.

Chapter Fifteen • 143
THE ROLE OF THE DIRECTOR OF ADVANCEMENT (CHIEF DEVELOPMENT OFFICER)
The Director of Advancement has a unique relationship with the governing board. Because both fundraising and the marketing of the organization are critical to its ability and opportunity to fulfill its mission, the person in this role works closely with the entire board.

CASE STUDY #12: *A Matter of Trust*   *151*
The development committee is a very important standing committee of the board. As such, the chair of the development committee must work closely with the CEO and director of development (chief development officer). Trust, respect, and support are characteristics that are essential for this relationship to thrive and to yield the best results to enhance the organization.

FOREWORD

If you have picked up this book, then I suspect you are someone who has an interest in understanding the dynamics of effective board management for a school or nonprofit organization. You may be someone who recently has been asked to take a seat on a volunteer board, and while you are passionate about the organization's mission, you are not so sure about stepping into the role of a board member. You may be someone who currently serves on a nonprofit board seeking to understand more completely what you should, and perhaps should not, be doing. You may be the president or executive director of a nonprofit trying to determine the appropriate boundaries between policy and effective organizational management. Or, you may be someone involved with a nonprofit organization wondering why there appears to be so much dysfunction between the board and the administration.

The path to successful nonprofit management is challenging. As a child, I loved stories about sea captains who left the shores of Europe or Asia to explore an uncharted world. They left full of hopes and expectations. They had a mission. But, most of the time, they did not have a reliable map. Along the way, they often found themselves off course. They faced titanic hurdles: unexpected storms, lack of adequate resources, and the death or illness of key personnel. At times and despite their best laid plans, they faced mutiny within their own ranks. What made the difference between those sea captains who achieved success and those who failed or perished largely centered on the captain's ability to adhere consistently to a set of guiding principles—principles that allowed the crew to do their jobs effectively while at the same time maintaining their confidence in the objectives of the mission.

What you will find when you read Bill Mott's *Super Boards* is a well-developed set of guiding principles for effective board management of schools and nonprofit organizations. Bill is uniquely suited to provide these important lessons. Recently, he published a highly successful book, *The Board Game*. It provided invaluable insight about board governance and how to manage the tension between the role of the board and the duties of the administration. Following on the success of *The Board Game*, Bill has lectured across the country to groups interested in learning about effective board management strategies for schools and nonprofit organizations. Bill also maintains a consulting business for nonprofits, providing advice on board structure, development, and decision making, as well as fundraising. In his career, Bill has valuable firsthand experience, having served as a board member with several nonprofit organizations and also having held executive level management positions with nonprofit institutions.

I have worked with numerous nonprofit organizations. Periodically, many of those organizations face unexpected difficulties. The challenges range from declining resources, the loss of a strong administrator, board-administration conflicts, or the need to adjust the organization's mission or focus. What I have seen is that the key to successfully managing any nonprofit is its board. Whenever a school or nonprofit achieves success, you can be certain that the board understands its role, follows a clear set of guiding principles, and provides confidence to those in charge of the day-to-day management. Many times an organization that appears in chaos or that is without direction is one that is led by a board that fails to adhere to a set of guiding principles and, as a result, undermines the confidence of those in charge of day-to-day management.

Super Boards provides a clear set of guiding principles. Using case studies and lessons learned from practical experience, Bill Mott delivers a well-developed resource for any school or nonprofit board to navigate the organization during both times of smooth sailing as well as times of unexpected challenges. Bill has provided what the sea captains of old did not have. Along with a set of experience-tested guiding principles, Bill has provided a reliable map.

Julian L. Bibb
Community & Nonprofit Leader
Attorney, Stites & Harbison, PLLC

Prologue

SIR CHRISTOPHER WREN: A STORY ABOUT MAKING A DIFFERENCE

In 1666 the Great Fire of London severely damaged London's famous St. Paul's Cathedral. King Charles II commissioned the renowned architect Sir Christopher Wren to rebuild the enormous structure, and construction finally began in 1675. One day as the great architect was walking through the construction site he encountered many stonecutters. Wren approached one of the men and asked, "What are you working on?" The stonecutter, perhaps not aware of to whom he was speaking, said, "I'm cutting stone—what does it look like I'm doing?" In other words, "Isn't it obvious?" Wren shook his head and moved on.

As he continued his survey of the site he spoke with another stonecutter and posed the same question. This man looked at the legendary architect and replied, "I'm working with you to build the greatest cathedral on earth." Wren thanked the man for his vision and passion for the work he was doing. Wren recognized that a positive attitude coupled with the skills needed to carry out the stonecutter's task resulted in seeing his role as contributing to something greater than himself.

This is a favorite story of mine. As I was writing this book, I thought it conveyed three valuable lessons regarding the nature of leadership and how that leadership makes such a mark on everyone connected with the leader and the organization.

The first of the three lessons has to do with shared vision. This unique story acknowledges the value of working together for a purpose greater than yourself. The second of the two stonecutters understood his role—that he was a part of something very important. He shared Christopher Wren's vision for doing something extraordinary. And being part of something extraordinary was a life-changing experience.

The second lesson contained in this story tells us something about attitude adjustment. Thomas Jefferson said, "Nothing can stop someone with the right attitude from achieving their goal; and nothing on earth can help someone with the wrong attitude." Clearly, stonecutter number one had an attitude problem! How you approach a task, the way you feel about yourself and those around you, can dramatically impact your success in achieving your goals. *Your attitude significantly defines who you are.* The first stonecutter Wren spoke with might have had the same skill level as the second stonecutter. However, without the passion, commitment, and dedication to participate in something exceptional like the rebuilding of St. Paul's he will not be as fulfilled as the second cutter.

The third lesson has everything to do with the recognition that making a difference is to have the self-awareness to truly have an impact. The second stonecutter knew full well his skills were going to make a difference on the appearance and strength of the cathedral. Making a difference goes to the very core of who we are and what we try to instill. Understanding that you are blessed and therefore bear some responsibility for stepping into the gap is filled with the idea that making a positive difference is worthy of our best.

The value and significance of working together to achieve the spectacular, the importance to the enterprise of having the most positive attitude possible, and the idea that you can make a difference and impact those around you, all resonate with the underlying theme of why it is so important for schools and organizations to seek to serve, to lead, and to inspire.

Introduction

INSPIRED LEADERSHIP
AND THE SPIRIT OF
COLLABORATION

"My words fly up, my thoughts remain below:
Words without thoughts never to heaven go."
—From *Hamlet* by William Shakespeare

Nonprofit organizations have always faced both unique challenges and amazing opportunities as they seek to live out
their mission and vision. These challenges and opportunities continue and arguably are more acute than before. The reasons are
many—the economic reality has certainly placed stress on many
nonprofit organizations. All the while, the incredible people who
work and lead these organizations do so with passion, commitment, and a renewed dedication to their profession. Where in this
panorama of challenges and opportunities do we find the board
of trustees? That is the central question for us to discover in this

1

book. It is their leadership and spirit of collaboration that we are seeking.

In the world of nonprofit books and other publications I am well aware that the actual and virtual bookshelves are crowded with literature addressing the topic of nonprofit governance and board development. The question then becomes, does my work add anything new or look at this topic in a different way that contributes to the dialogue? It is a valid question. I recently read an impressive new biography about Thomas Jefferson. There are numerous books written about Jefferson. Did we need yet another biography? After reading this latest biography I would conclude that we absolutely did! Why? Because the author takes a fresh look and perspective of the great man and shines a light on his genius that otherwise might not have been explored.

In this book I have tried to achieve something different—to focus attention on several issues that serve to reveal and separate organizations that have strong, dynamic boards that include leaders whose genuine purpose is to be the best possible board member. My five specific goals include:

1. To describe and discuss the transformational responsibilities of the committee on trustees in such a way as to elevate their mission to recruit, retain, educate, and evaluate the board.

2. To introduce a component to the discussion of board responsibilities that solidifies the all-important relationship that board members must have with one another and with the organization's leadership. This Covenant Agreement is a document some

organizations possess but do not give the attention needed for excellence.

3. To think differently and more openly about governance and to create a culture that understands that serving on the board is serious work, but that we find a place for joy in the excellence that is the capstone of the experience.

4. To assure leaders that the status quo is not a "death sentence." An organization's, and specifically a board's, ability to function at the highest level can move from bad to good and good to great. It is possible and worth the effort (perhaps the sacrifices) required to move forward.

5. To reinforce the central theme that although the board of trustees of an organization consists of many individuals, it must, once a decision is made, act and speak with one voice.

As referenced above with the quotation from Shakespeare, this book is to be thoughtful and intentional in its approach to the topic of how nonprofit governing boards can genuinely strive to be excellent in carrying out their tasks and responsibilities. Words alone are not enough—but the right words, coupled with right actions, will make a positive difference and have the greatest influence.

Leadership is defined in different ways by different people with different perspectives. Here is the way I define it: *Leadership is the ability of someone or a group to encourage and to inspire others. It is the ability to discover the best in someone and, through encouragement and inspiration, to bring out the best in individuals or groups. It is also the recognition that relationships matter, particularly the relationship between the CEO and the board of trustees.* It is through this lens that we shine a spotlight on creating and sustaining super boards.

As in my book *The Board Game*, the ultimate achievement is raising the issues and engaging in meaningful discussion. That is where the magic may be found. My hope is that you will discover something new, different, meaningful, or helpful as you read, reflect, and act on the pages that follow.

Chapter One

VOLUNTEER BOARDS— VOLUNTEER LEADERS

Volunteer boards are an essential part of every nonprofit organization. They are required by state and federal law and therefore play a central role in the organization's ability to achieve its mission and vision. When boards are utilized effectively, they can be a major asset and a source for support not found elsewhere. However, if proper leadership and direction are absent, volunteer boards can be a roadblock and actually prevent an organization from achieving its goals. At the beginning of the process of examining the governing board, here are some of the issues that should be priorities:

- Focus on board responsibilities and begin to make a list of what constitutes a dynamic and inspired board. How does the organization's mission and vision impact board responsibilities and priorities?

- Analyze the current board in terms of their effectiveness and develop criteria such as: fundraising, professional skills, diversity, advocacy, attendance, participation, etc. Discover what is working well that should be supported and what is not working that should be improved or eliminated.

- Decide what mix of talents make the board most effective. What are the needs that can be addressed by talent and skills represented on the board? Do we really understand the needs and do we have the capability of attracting these kinds of individuals?

- Consider statements such as *The Covenant Agreement* or adopt *The Governance Promise*, something that provides clear understanding as to the importance of the relationship between the staff and the board. These guiding principles can set expectations and be a road map for current and future board members.

- Develop a manual that includes such information as:
  1. List of current board members, including contact information
  2. Mission statement
  3. Brief history of the organization
  4. Marketing and fundraising materials
  5. Meeting calendar for the year
  6. Minutes from the previous year

7. Other relevant material that would assist a new board member

BOARD OF TRUSTEES VS. BOARD OF TRUST: ONE BOARD—ONE VOICE

Perhaps it is only a matter of semantics, but I believe it is worth making note of the distinction between a term we use widely and probably give little thought to the inferences and a term that is used much more sparingly. The board of trustees suggests a group of individuals who act and perform their roles and responsibilities as a group. The Board of *Trust* suggests that this is a group who act and perform their responsibilities as one cohesive unit. I believe that this is not simply semantics but rather a statement about the true meaning of *trusteeship*. Working together with one voice is, or certainly should be, the way in which the best and most effective boards function. Throughout this book I refer to the board of trustees, but my hope is that these individuals have come together for the greater good and truly function as a Board of Trust.

Chapter Two

RECRUITING INSPIRED BOARD MEMBERS

Recruiting and maintaining the most inspired board members possible is the joint responsibility of the board's committee on trustees (the most-often used name for this committee), all board members, and the organization's staff. Each of these two components has an important task when considering who to add to the board. The needs of the organization must be clear and carefully articulated to a prospective trustee.

The recruitment process is critical. If done in a haphazard manner that lacks focus, the organization will not be able to attract the people most needed to serve on the board. Here are some factors to consider:

- *Gender:* It is important to have diversity on the board. Representation on the board should reflect the makeup of the organization's constituency. It is not only the politically right thing to do; it will also enhance the organization in numerous ways.

- *Age:* A range of ages most likely is a healthy way to build the board. All too often boards are made up of older people. Generally a range of ages adds different perspectives and depth.

- *Occupation:* Does the board include expertise and experience in areas that will be helpful? There is value in having different occupations represented; just be sure that you have members with knowledge of finance, marketing, facilities, and other beneficial areas.

- *Ethnicity:* Ethnic diversity adds to the board and to the organization in meaningful ways. Having representation from different ethnic groups demonstrates an understanding of the various contributions that can be enormously constructive and beneficial.

- *Recommendation source:* Is the person making the recommendation someone whose opinion is valued and who has the best interest of the organization, as opposed to someone who wants to pad their particular agenda?

- *Other board affiliations and interests:* Potential board members have their own sphere of influence—which can extremely helpful. Be sure you capture this information in the recruitment process. If a prospective board member has served or is currently serving on another board, that information may reveal his or her ability to be an effective and supportive board member.

- *Strengths and specific areas of contribution:* A matrix identifying needs and strengths allows the board to be intentional about what skills and abilities are most needed. For example, if a capital campaign is on the horizon, those with knowledge of fundraising, construction, and facilities management might be sought.

The process of securing a commitment from a prospective board member is one that requires great care. Here are several examples of ways to determine the compatibility of a prospect with the organization and staff:

Invite the person to attend an event.

An appropriate priority in recruitment is to find out all you can about a prospective board member. One of the ways to do this is to invite the person to attend an event—either at the location of the organization or elsewhere. The purpose is to begin to introduce the prospective board member (assuming they are not already completely familiar with the organization) to key staff, donors, volunteers, and, of course, other board members.

Seek the candidate's assistance or input on a committee.

Many nonprofit organizations have great success by including non-trustees on board committees. The organization may be seeking the input from someone with specific expertise. The organization may recognize the value of someone who may not have the time commitment needed to serve on the board. And, the organization may ask a non-trustee with the idea of looking at the person as being a potential trustee in the future.

Invite the candidate to meet other board members, the CEO, and the development and marketing staff.

Beyond meeting people at an event it is very important that prospective trustees have opportunities to get to know the organization's leadership. This is important for several reasons, not the least of which is that it speeds up the process of becoming more informed about the mission, vision, and programs of the organization.

Offer a tour of the facilities.

Part of the candidate's becoming informed is to see and tour the organization's facilities. It demonstrates a commitment by making the effort to physically see the organization—it is a component of increasing their knowledge of the organization.

A member of the committee on trustees (perhaps the chair) and the CEO should invite the candidate to meet them. A personal invitation to meet these two individuals should be a strong signal that the organization takes the process of adding trustees very seriously. Is this process time-consuming? Yes. Is this process essential to the future of the organization? Absolutely—recruiting the best possible trustee will have an enormous impact!

Following the candidate's agreement to serve and approval by the full board, a separate letter of welcome should be sent from the board chair and CEO. The letter should outline arrangements for the board orientation session.

"We have an opening on our board..."

Linda and her husband had moved into their condominium just a few months ago. They loved the location and the fact that their new yard was a small one. Linda enjoyed gardening but especially enjoyed having a confined space to tend her garden. She also really enjoyed the fact that one of the responsibilities of the homeowner's association was mowing and landscaping not only the common ground of the complex but also each individual yard. This enabled Linda to focus her outside energy on having the nicest garden possible.

One morning as she was outside working, a neighbor walked by and stopped to talk with her. Linda had never met him, but he was nice and very complimentary of the appearance of the garden and the overall exterior of her condominium. As they were discussing the issue of plants, trees, and the importance of such matters, he suddenly shifted gears. He unexpectedly announced that, "We have an opening on the homeowner's association board and wondered if you would be interested in being a member?"

Linda looked at him a long moment and thought to herself, *Is this the most effective way to recruit board members? How serious could this board be when he is asking someone he just met and knows nothing about?* Finally she replied, "Thank you for asking, but that is not something I can do right now." Without missing a beat her new friend responded, "Well, I know there will be another opening in a few months. Perhaps that would be a more convenient time." She noted he said this more as a statement rather than a question. She smiled and decided it best not to react to this. After a few more minutes of idle conversation he said he had to be going but that it was nice meeting her.

QUESTIONS FOR DISCUSSION

1. *What is your initial reaction to this encounter?*

2. *What motivated the man to ask Linda to join the board?*

3. *What is your opinion of his approach?*

4. *Do you believe he was authorized to extend that offer?*

5. *What does this episode tell you about the homeowner's association board?*

6. *What did Linda's reaction tell you about her?*

7. *What should have happened?*

Chapter Three

TRAINING AND ORIENTATION FOR BOARD MEMBERS

In many nonprofit organizations several board members typically or often join the board at a specified time of the year, thus creating a "class" of new board members who begin and potentially are re-elected or rotate off at the same time.

ORIENTATION

Regardless of the number of new members coming on the board an orientation session is essential for the reasons described below:

- An orientation session introduces the new board member(s) to officers, key staff members, and other new board members. If they have already met, this will be an opportunity to get to know them and initiate a relationship with them.

- An orientation session should review the history of the organization. Never assume a new trustee is particularly familiar with the organization. Of course, there may be new trustees who know the organization very well. However, even they will benefit from a history lesson.

- An orientation session should describe and review the committee structure of the board. Committee assignments may be made at the orientation session or soon after. As so much work is accomplished through committees, they will be an essential part of the orientation session.

- An orientation session should provide the new board member with a manual, or the documentation and materials should be sent electronically. Such a manual should include all pertinent material that the member would need to know in order to be the most effective board member possible.

- An orientation session should set the tone to establish responsibilities and expectations.

- An orientation session will allow the new board member to feel welcome and recognized as a contributing member of the organization from the beginning. An orientation session dramatically reduces the "learning curve" for a new trustee.

TRAINING

There are numerous ways to effectively train or provide ongoing education for members of your board of trustees. Research and best practices collide with the fundamental truth that boards that are better trained and that engage in continuous professional development are significantly more effective in their role and, therefore, are better positioned to contribute to the board and the organization they are serving.

Training can occur in a variety of settings and circumstances. Here are a few to keep in mind:

Board Retreat

The board retreat is a time-tested and proven way in which training as well as evaluation of the board can occur. Topics for retreats can vary but usually fall into a few general categories:

- *Strategic Planning.* Often a board will use a retreat setting to initiate a strategic planning process. Once the process has been completed, the board may use a retreat to conclude the strategic planning process. Both retreats can be highly effective and focused ways in which to address the strategic direction of the organization.

- *Board Evaluation.* The board may see a retreat as a way to determine its own effectiveness. Often each trustee completes an evaluation instrument and the results are then shared and discussed during the retreat. Again, a retreat setting can provide focus and purpose by encouraging the board to clearly understand, accept, and carry out their responsibilities. Chapter 11 and Appendix I include an evaluation instrument that may be helpful to your organization.

- *Fundraising Campaign.* The decision by an organization to consider a major fundraising program usually requires extensive planning and the formulation of that plan and the steps necessary to implement the plan and deliberations held in a retreat setting may well reveal strengths and concerns regarding the plan.

- *Programmatic Initiatives.* Nonprofit organizations often have a variety of programs and services they provide as a part of their mission and vision. The board retreat can be a venue for dialogue as to whether additions, deletions, or changes to programs should result. The genesis of fundraising campaigns and programmatic review may well be the strategic planning process.

- *General Business of the Organization.* Board retreats may also be similar to a regular meeting in terms of the agenda but may take place in a setting that allows the board to bond and build stronger relationships over a more extended period of time beyond what a regular meeting would allow.

The experience of a board retreat is often enhanced by the presence and guidance of a facilitator, or consultant. This individual should be brought in as an independent resource capable of providing experience, perspective, wisdom, and respect to the entire proceeding. Having such a person leading the process tends to allow everyone—board, CEO, staff— more freedom to actively participate in the discussion. Every nonprofit organization should conduct retreats and should budget for a consultant to help achieve the results needed for success.

Seminar or Workshop

Many nonprofit organizations and associations at the national, regional, state, and even local level offer all manner of workshop and seminar opportunities for trustees. There is an enormous emphasis placed on these opportunities because of the recognition that governance is so significant to the organization and that board development is linked directly to achieving potential.

A critical aspect of seminars and workshops is the opportunity for both the board chair and CEO to participate together. There is little that is more important than the chair and CEO to hear, discuss, and question the same message about the impact of these two leaders on organizational greatness.

While more such opportunities would be helpful, the real challenge is for the board chair and members of the board to discover how important and valuable these sessions are.

What we need is for more professional associations to provide more opportunities to discuss board development issues and for there to be more opportunities for CEOs and board chairs to attend together on issues of mutual interest.

Leadership Coaching

Often overlooked and not completely understood is the opportunity for boards, board chairs, and CEOs to participate in leadership coaching. This "personal trainer" concept can be enormously beneficial to the individuals involved and can lead to better self-awareness, stronger relationships, and organizational enhancements.

Inspired boards are ones that work well together. Board education through retreats, seminars, workshops, and coaching is an enormously important investment an organization can make in its future.

CASE STUDY #2

Shifting Expectations

The interview had gone well. Robert was not very surprised. He had had many phone conversations and e-mail communications with the chair of the search committee. It was obvious and gratifying that Robert and Carl had already established a very positive relationship. Robert was excited about the prospect of becoming the head of school at this well-known if fairly new independent school. If it worked out, this would be his third, and probably last, school where he would serve as the Head. Robert would turn 53 in the fall.

Carl and the entire search committee had been very positive. Robert was anxious to hear as much as possible about the working relationship between the head of school and board. He asked every question he could think of and wanted to be as certain as possible regarding expectations and how his performance would be evaluated. Carl seemed to be very positive and receptive to Robert's inquiries.

A few weeks later Robert was offered the position and he and Carl discussed major points to put into a letter of agreement and ultimately a contract. Robert should have seen some problems brewing when the draft of his contract was over twenty pages! Alarms did go off but he was not overly concerned with the length or the language in the document.

Shifting Expectations

At the end of the first year everything changed. For personal reasons Carl had to leave the board and the transition to the new chair had been awkward. Don had been a member of the board but in the last twelve months he had been elevated to vice chair and treasurer. His priorities and expectations for Robert were very different than those of Carl's. And suddenly, Don was the new chair!

Mostly unknown to Robert when he arrived at the school was a significant financial commitment with a schedule that called for a million-dollar payment eighteen months after he began as head of school. Robert had been told that the payment was being renegotiated and that if Robert could reduce the amount by half that would signal the bankers of the efforts the school was making. He was determined to reduce this by more if possible.

During the eighteen-month period with Robert's leadership and experience as a fundraiser, he had managed to lead efforts that resulted in over $800,000 given toward the million-dollar goal. Robert had assumed that the board would view this as a very positive move in ultimately reaching the goal. But he failed to recognize Don's insistence that all of the money be committed. With no notice Robert's expectations had been shifted. With no warning he would be evaluated on a goal that was completely unrealistic.

QUESTIONS FOR DISCUSSION

1. *What red flags can you see regarding Robert's contract?*

2. *Why are transitions between two board chairs so often difficult?*

3. *What conclusions can you draw regarding what Robert was told by Carl and others on the finance committee?*

4. *What is your opinion regarding what to share with a prospective candidate?*

Chapter Four

THE CRITICAL ROLE
OF THE COMMITTEE
ON TRUSTEES

The nonprofit board of trustees is critical to the effective operation of the organization—not because the board has day-to-day oversight but rather because of their fiduciary, mission, vision, and strategic direction responsibilities. Board members come to their roles as trustees from a variety of perspectives, backgrounds, and constituencies and therefore require training and education as to what constitutes being a valuable and valued trustee.

In many organizations, the board has a standing committee often known as the committee on trustees. This committee is typically charged with the following responsibilities:

Identifying Prospective Trustees

One of the most important roles for the board of trustees is to develop an ongoing list of prospective trustees—individuals who can bring the skills needed to provide the support and skills to advance the organization. This list should be compiled with input from a range of sources and reviewed in anticipation of recruiting the next group or class of trustees. The committee on trustees should meet well in advance of any deadline to ensure that a thorough review can take place to prioritize board candidates.

Developing the Process and Plan to Recruit Trustees

The process of recruiting trustees must be strategic and intentional. A genuine action plan that has the steps necessary to engage those most suited to contribute is required. Such a plan should include:

- Who and when the initial contact is made

- Setting up a meeting to discuss being on the board

- Determining who is most compatible with prospective trustee

- Selecting an appropriate setting for the visit to occur

- Following up and establishing the next action steps

- Creating a welcome strategy

These steps may seem to be too much, perhaps more than may be necessary. Each organization has to set the right tone, attitude, and methodology to ensure the process is yielding the candidates most needed. Every organization will approach this task in a way that reflects their organizational culture. However, every organization must understand that these elements, whatever way they are carried out, must be included when recruiting.

Meeting with Each Prospective Trustee

This is a mandatory and critical step in trustee recruiting. All too often the board nominating committee, as some are referred to, believes it is unnecessary to actually hold a face-to-face meeting with a prospective trustee. There are four reasons why so many boards make this strategic mistake:

1. Do they believe that anyone and everyone is clamoring to be on their board?

2. Are they unaware that competition for volunteer board members is actually intense?

3. Are they lazy and simply waited until the last minute to discover that it's now too late?

4. Have they not been trained or in some way guided to understand how dangerous this is?

The elements of this meeting in terms of *when, where, who,* and *what* will determine how valuable it will ultimately be. *When* of course has to do with the timing of when new trustees begin their service—typically found in the bylaws. *Where* the meeting takes should be casual and friendly while at the same time including a serious tone—a breakfast or lunch is usually an excellent venue. *Who* should meet with the new trustee? It depends, but the chair of the committee on trustees, the organization's CEO, should be there, and perhaps the chair of the board. Possibly someone on the board who is close to the prospective trustee may also be included. *What* is conveyed is the final piece of the puzzle. The conversation must include:

- Information about the organization (included in packet)

- List of trustees (included in packet)

- Promotional materials (included in packet)

- A time for questions and answers specifically designed to determine the attitude and perspective of the person being recruited

- Stories and "case studies" designed to reveal expectations and best practices

- Specific discussion of fundraising and its importance to the organization along with the role of each trustee

- Discussion of board culture that makes clear where the board stands on issues such as conflict of interest, confidentiality, and hidden agendas

Developing an Orientation Session for New Trustees

If the committee on trustees has done their job in recruiting the best trustees, then the orientation session has every possibility of being successful. If they have not been able to attract excellent trustees, but only those trustees who come with an agenda or trustees who possess a poor attitude toward their role, then an orientation session will make little difference.

The orientation session ideally reinforces what the new trustee heard when being recruited. It should address a range of issues including:

- Role of CEO

- Relationship between CEO and board

- Meeting schedule

- Committee structure

- Bylaws

- Minutes

- Expectations

Providing Continuing Education of Trustees Through Retreats and Other Professional Development Opportunities

One of the aspects of board development that lacks attention are trustees not being encouraged to participate in professional development opportunities—conferences, workshops, and seminars devoted to topics and issues that support trustees doing their job better. It is critical that trustees be engaged in these types of activities and be on the lookout for opportunities to improve and be better board members.

Many boards conduct retreats and often on an annual basis. Retreats come in a variety of shapes and sizes—meaning there is no single model that works best. Here are some effective ways to conduct a retreat:

- Hold a retreat annually.

- If possible, meet in a location away from the organization's headquarters.

- Meet in a location that is as free from distractions and disruptions as possible.

- Build into the agenda time away to work on team-building, including time for fellowship and occasions for socializing.

- Focus discussion on long-range visioning (strategic planning) issues, fundraising/advancement/marketing issues, major programmatic initiatives, facility priorities, or financial matters.

- Develop an action plan and assignments resulting from the retreat.

- Set aside time to conduct a board meeting and possibly committee meetings.

Working in Partnership with the Organization's CEO (Executive Director) on All of the Above

Although not universally true, in many 501(c)(3) organizations the CEO, or executive director, is considered to be the only employee of the board of trustees. The success of this reporting relationship is the key in organizational success. It is the foundation on which the organization thrives. In its absence the viability of the organization is significantly diminished.

The capacity to move the organization from this relationship to a true partnership demonstrates an understanding of how this can transform the organization. At the heart of this partnership is the realization that the CEO and board chair must collaborate and establish a model as a way of working together. There may be nothing more important than this single issue!

Governance by E-Mail

Sam stared at the e-mail and was somewhat stunned by what he was seeing. He certainly knew that there were decisions that could be made by e-mail—the absence of the board actually being in the same room to make a decision. But a decision like this seemed to him to require a genuine discussion and not merely a response to a vote by e-mail.

The e-mail was about a trustee, Ted, who was proposing to build and completely fund a new indoor football practice complex at the independent school where Sam served as a trustee. Such a facility would be wonderful to have. However, this was not a priority and not something in the strategic plan. Ted seemed not to have any concern for what was included in the strategic plan but rather for the school to have what he thought was most needed.

Ted's offer seemed too good to be true. He volunteered to construct the facility and completely pay for it—regardless of cost. But there was a catch—the school would have no opportunity to determine the appearance of the facility. Ted was a contractor and knew best about how to fit it in to the rest of the campus. To Sam this appeared problematic. The board would have no oversight into any aspect of this construction project estimated at about $2 million.

The e-mail, sent from the chair of the board, was asking for the board to vote on whether or not to move forward on this construction project. It was clear that the executive committee and building and grounds committee had already voted in favor of the project. In the end Sam went along with his trustee colleagues and voted in favor of the project.

Two years later the building was complete. While it was not compatible with other campus buildings it could have been worse. Because this project became the priority, capital projects in the strategic plan were put on hold. Although Ted had repeatedly promised that the building would not cost the school any money, cost overruns were over $100,000, and Ted was very slow to complete his commitment. In fact, the auditors were raising questions as to whether or not the school should write off as a loss the money he still owed toward completing the project.

QUESTIONS FOR DISCUSSION

1. *What is your opinion about voting by e-mail?*

2. *How should the chair and the executive committee address trustees who have agendas?*

3. *Why do you believe Sam voted with the other trustees?*

4. *Although this project was not part of the strategic direction, should it have been considered?*

5. *How do you believe the school should have responded when it became obvious Ted had little intention paying what was owed?*

6. *Should the bylaws be consulted regarding how a vote is taken?*

7. *Do you believe someone like Ted would have benefitted from participating in a trustee workshop?*

Chapter Five

DEFINING KEY RESPONSIBILITIES OF THE BOARD

As the governing body for the nonprofit organization the board of trustees has numerous responsibilities, some of which are mandated by the organization's articles of incorporation and bylaws. As with most topics and issues addressed in this book, there are numerous lists and definitions as to a board's role and responsibilities. These include the following:

1. Set forth the organization's mission, vision, and purpose.

Perhaps best known and most discussed is this responsibility. The mission, vision, and purpose is the organization's reason for being and strategic articulation of who it is and who it wants to become. This is the collective responsibility of all board members and should be well understood by each member.

2. Partner with the CEO and work intentionally to ensure this person's success.

This may be the least understood responsibility of the board. All too often referred to as the "hire and fire" statement, what the board should strive for is an authentic spirit of partnership, collaboration, understanding, and support. This does not preclude the reporting nature of the CEO and the fact that the board has only one employee. The significance of expressing the relationship in this way makes clear what is really at stake—working together is central to this relationship, and this is a responsibility of the entire board.

3. Ensure that vigorous strategic planning is a priority.

All planning should be strategic! The considered and deliberate way to move forward is a significant priority of the board. This takes on different formats for different organizations. The intent, however, must remain constant—to review where you have been, determine where you want to go, and create the steps needed to make that change. Often the direct responsibility of a strategic planning committee, this group has oversight of the process. All committees and all board members have a stake to ensure the process is active, meaningful, and inclusive.

4. Ensure adequate financial resources are in place to operate the organization.

Financial solvency and sustainability are obviously keys to the organization's viability. Nonprofit does not mean "no money"! From the perspective of the board, the treasurer and the finance committee have the specific charge for ensuring the budget is balanced and that the financial records are in order—and confirmed by an independent auditing process. However, the fiduciary responsibility is every trustee's responsibility. I once worked with a trustee who believed that every board member at one time during their tenure should sit in on meetings of the finance committee to get a better understanding of the issues faced by the organization. Not a bad idea.

We speak today of transparency and must understand that not only is it the right thing to do but helps assure the constituency that the organization has nothing to hide and is operating according to appropriate accounting guidelines and practices. This does not imply that you post your budget on your web site or that you allow anyone and everyone to look at whatever their particular issue or concern might be. What it does mean is that you listen to such a request and determine whether or not it is legitimate.

I once had a parent of the school I headed asking to see the budget. When I inquired what specifically they were seeking to learn, I discovered they wanted to complain about a particular department being underfunded. That is not the transparency I refer to.

5. Make giving to the organization a priority.

This is one of those issues that never fails to surface and never fails to be controversial. If someone is a member of the board of trustees then I believe giving to that organization should be a philanthropic priority—at least during the time the person is serving as a trustee. Period! No exceptions. Two things are at issue here. First, it is the responsibility of the committee on trustees to make it crystal clear what the expectations are with respect to trustee giving. This must be done before someone is asked to join the board, *not* after. Second, make certain that everyone is not required to contribute the same amount, but rather to be as generous as possible given that individual's circumstances.

6. Ensure that all resources are managed effectively.

All resources encompass everything including endowment performance, physical plant, budget, audit, and the operation of the business office. The expectation is that there are people on the board that have the knowledge and expertise to understand endowment performance, managing the facilities, including depreciation of assets and the other issues critical to a successful, sustainable operation. Again, the committee on trustees must recognize this need and find the right people who can provide wisdom in these often complex areas. While the business manager (CFO) reports to the CEO, this person works closely with the board treasurer and chair of the finance committee—often this is the same individual. The business manager must possess the experience and financial expertise to converse knowledgeably with the treasurer. Nowhere is trust, collaboration, and respect more needed than in the working relationship between these two.

7. Do not engage in conflicts of interest.

Often discussed but seldom understood is the definition of "conflict of interest." Such behavior is unacceptable, unethical, and erodes trust among everyone familiar with the organization.

Simply stated, conflict of interest exists when a board member joins the board with the purpose of seeking to gain an advantage as a board member by securing business or favors that are unfairly or inappropriately obtained. It is a complex and frequently misunderstood occurrence.

Two examples seem appropriate. The first involves a board member who is also a contractor. The organization is renovating a building and this contractor is one of the bidders for this job. The organization reviews several bids—including the one from the board member. Is this a conflict of interest? No. The board member was not seeking to receive special treatment or an unfair advantage by virtue of serving on the board.

The second example involves a board member who is also a stockbroker. This individual joins the board and hopes that by doing so he can align himself to make other trustees his clients. Is this a conflict of interest? Yes. This trustee is using his position to influence others on the board to do business. Further, if the broker trustee does in fact do business with other trustees, to keep that business in tact he supports their positions to maintain that business relationship. That is an enormous conflict of interest and has the potential to damage the organization.

8. In conjunction with the CEO, monitor the organization's programs and services.

It is not the board's responsibility to manage the day-to-day operation of the organization. It is, however, a trustee's responsibility to be attentive to the programs and services the organization provides. This is an area in which the trustee's relationship with the CEO becomes an advantage. Becoming well informed with programs and services will make you a better and valued trustee.

9. Enhance the organization's public image.

While not often considered a responsibility of the board, the public perception of the organization is in fact the responsibility of everyone closely connected—which includes the board of trustees. It may be both appropriate and helpful to have on the board individuals with expertise and experience in the areas of marketing, branding, communications, and public relations.

10. Embrace the concept of confidentiality.

It is not enough to say the words—you have to walk the walk. In other words, this concept must be clearly articulated as an expectation. Nonprofit organizations and their boards of trustees are not immune to gossip, rumor spreading, or other forms of improper communication. Most of us understand the TV ad campaign that states, "What happens in Vegas, stays in Vegas!" The work of the board and the discussions and decisions that result are not to be shared in a public way. To be sure, certain public organizations are subject to laws that determine what must be public record. That is not the issue here.

How do you reconcile transparency while at the same time keeping confidential certain information? As a 501(c)(3), nonprofit organization, you are well within both your rights and responsibilities to not share certain information. The board of trustees has the legal and fiduciary responsibility to manage and direct the organization as they see fit—according to the limitations of the charter and bylaws.

Someone once told me about an organization's board chair that began every meeting admonishing the board about the importance of confidentiality. The board *and* the board chair did not adhere to this warning and had the reputation of being known for sharing information about all manner of subjects—including information on individuals. This type of behavior is unethical and highly inappropriate. If you talk the talk, you must walk the walk.

11. Evaluate the board's performance.

All too often boards do an inadequate job evaluating their own performance or effectiveness. In fact, many boards do not do this at all. And when they do it is anecdotal with little data of value that has any impact on anything. There are numerous ways in which evaluation can be accomplished but none of it matters if the board chair and the officers of the board place little or no value in the process.

It is more than a little ironic that the same board that refuses to evaluate how well they do what they are supposed to be doing is the same group who will place significance on evaluating the CEO of the organization. In spite of what the board thinks, it works both ways! And because it works both ways, the organization is the beneficiary of this way of conducting business. The board must evaluate what they do and how they perform.

- - -

Above all, the board's responsibility is primarily a policy-making one. In smaller organizations where there is a smaller staff, the board may find itself more involved in the organization's operation. However, the board should still be cognizant of the fact that their role greatly differs from that of the staff.

CASE STUDY #4

Bully on Board

Board bullying may be defined when a board member attempts to threaten and intimidate the organization's leader or someone on his or her staff. The board member is using his or her position of authority to belittle and place in an awkward position the organization's executive director.

Walt and Phil did not look forward to visiting Carl at his office. The purpose of the visit was to solicit Carl for his gift to the campaign. Actually, the purpose of the visit was to follow up on a gift solicitation made earlier by Walt and another member of the board. Walt, the organization's CEO, and Phil, the vice president for development, were calling on Carl, a member of the board for the past three years. To Walt and Phil, Carl represented everything that gave a bad name to trustees. He was arrogant, deceitful, talked much more than he listened, and never conceived he was wrong about any issue.

The conversation opened with numerous pleasantries and an assurance of a gift—including, however, much criticism of the wording on the gift pledge card.

Soon the conversation turned to the recent board election. Walt and Phil expressed genuine excitement about the new members' potential and looked forward to working with them. Carl's response to their excitement was both unexpected and totally inappropriate. He remarked, "The new members will be supportive (of Walt and Phil) for a year, but if you do not produce in terms of successful fundraising, they will turn on you." Carl's arrogance and willingness to speak on behalf of the new board members without having any idea of what he was saying seemed both ridiculous and threatening. Was this a threat? Was this a warning? Did the board member have inside information about the new board members that would lead him to make this statement? Or was he merely stating his own bias as to how he felt about the organization's leader? Walt knew it would do little good to argue or respond. He did ask Carl, "Do you believe that there is something that we are not doing but should be doing?" There was no response to his question.

This story stands out because I think it reflects and reveals the complete lack of sensitivity and understanding that Carl has of his role. This type of bullying is one in which someone uses their position in an improper way. Whether intended or not, the statement by the board member was threatening to the executive. This was in every way unacceptable behavior. As a private conversation it would be difficult for such a conversation to make its way to the board chair. But it should have. Walt should have gone to the chair—not as someone telling on or whining about the mistreatment but rather about unacceptable behavior from someone who is supposed to be a partner. And the board chair should have confronted Carl about what kind of communication is appropriate behavior. Certainly, confrontation of this kind is unpleasant, but there is no alternative.

What we know to be the most effective are board members who partner with the leadership of the organization. Working together to achieve common goals, board members and staff leaders are responsible for the stability and future of the organization. Bullying is best avoided if the committee on trustees does their job and selects the best possible trustees.

QUESTIONS FOR DISCUSSION

1. *Do you know trustees like Carl?*

2. *Would you have reacted in the same way as Walt and Phil?*

3. *Why do you believe Carl treats people this way?*

4. *If you were the board chair, describe how you have handled this situation.*

5. *What can the recruitment process do to prevent this from happening?*

Chapter Six

THE FIVE MOST IMPORTANT RESPONSIBILITIES OF THE BOARD CHAIR

Every time I see the "wag more, bark less" bumper sticker, it brings a smile to my face. There are several reasons for this. First, it is probably an indicator that the driver has a pretty positive attitude toward life. Second, he is probably a "dog person"—which is a good thing. And third, it symbolizes that being positive and happy probably trumps being mean and grumpy. I think about my dog Roscoe, a world-famous dachshund, and his wag-to-bark ratio. He wags a lot—even when he barks he's still wagging his tail. So Roscoe is happy even when he is barking. It is a lesson for all of us. In this context, it is a lesson for all nonprofit trustees—and board chairs. Your attitude regarding your responsibilities will determine your success in carrying them out!

Nonprofit board chairs have numerous responsibilities

and these are often described and debated in abundant books, articles, blogs, online discussions, etc. I am sure all are important contributions. However, the single factor that overcomes all others is to have a great relationship with the CEO (executive director, president, head of school, etc.) of the organization. In the absence of this, the organization is likely to struggle to realize the full potential of their mission and vision. Given this issue's importance as the pretext for this topic, what then constitutes the board chair's five most important responsibilities?

1. Encourage the board to work together.

The idea of the board of trustees working together for the good of the organization seems to be a given. Unfortunately, the reality is often very different. Politics, egos, agendas, conflicts of interest, and ongoing disagreements get in the way of working together. One of the chair's responsibilities is to bring order out of this chaos and remind all board members why they are there—to govern in such a way as to act in the best interest of the organization. Differences of opinion? Certainly they are not only a fact of life but may result in making the best decision. Working together, however, will result in what is best about serving on a board of trustees.

2. Insist that interactions and relationships be not only civil but also positive as in having a positive attitude even when disagreements arise.

Our society has gone from "reasonable people can disagree" to "let's trash and demonize anyone who disagrees with me" mentality. (Thus, the need for the "wag more, bark less" reminder.)

Why has this happened? Is it a reflection of the attitude and rancor that seems to be the way many elected officials behave? Are there other contributing factors? We seem to have forgotten that we have much more in common than different—yet we focus too much on the differences. This attitude will *not* serve the organization but will create a spirit of divisiveness that surely leads to stalemate. The board chair must set the tone and have the highest expectations for all members. The chair must articulate the power of positive teamwork as the most reasonable and appropriate way to move forward.

3. Position the CEO as a leader worthy of respect and trust.

The board chair and the CEO must be a team and must work together for the good of the organization. The chair has to be responsible for insuring that all trustees see the CEO as a person whom they respect—an individual they believe has the leadership skills needed to make a positive impact. The chair should demonstrate to all trustees that the CEO exhibits character and integrity and that they are worthy of the trustees' collective and individual support. And the CEO provides the leadership needed to serve in the top administrative and management role. Not a "mutual admiration society," but rather a genuine sense of working together to communicate a compelling shared vision for the organization's future. Different roles and responsibilities, but united in outcome.

4. Ensure that the Board's focus is on core responsibilities of mission, strategy, policy, and planning.

The word micromanaging (also see number 5) has almost become a cliché for nonprofit organizations. It occurs so often we have almost become numb to its impact. One of the most fundamental misuses of a board's responsibility is to forget why they are the Board and what their responsibilities include. There is a process that if followed can mean great things. The magic is in that process where the board is educated and trained as to their unique role and the value in that role for the organization. Why is it that boards decide they should *run* the organization, which inevitably leads to the *ruin* of an organization? When the board adds that *I*, they make a huge mistake! If the board believes there is an absence in leadership, then the members should address that situation rather than try to involve themselves in operational matters. The board's role is strategic, not day-to-day. The chair must be the cheerleader for insuring that the focus stays on the issues the members are charged with fulfilling.

5. Resist every temptation to meddle or micromanage any member of the senior staff.

Certain levels of communication are needed as a part of the structure of the organization. Board and staff are often a part of the committee structure and an exchange of ideas in this arena is encouraged. However, there are too many examples of board members going beyond this and using their role as trustees to intimidate and in some cases bully or threaten staff members. This is totally inappropriate and unethical. Almost without fail, the trustee will claim to be innocent of any wrongdoing. This is when the chair is obligated to establish the boundaries of interaction and communication. The CEO is not in a position to effectively handle this matter because the trustees are the body they report to. It is the chair who communicates with clarity and purpose as to what is acceptable.

- - -

Being the board chair is a challenging task. However, with this level of leadership comes the responsibility to lead! And that may mean taking difficult stands and making difficult decisions in order to do what is best for the organization *and* support the CEO when that is the action required. The challenges are great—the rewards, greater. This is the type of leadership every board should require of its chair. Having the right leader with the right attitude is a "game changer." Can board chairs wag and bark at the same time? In other words, can they be both positive while sometimes having to be tough on their trustee peers? Wagging more, barking less—not a bad philosophy. I think I'll buy a bumper sticker. Roscoe would like that.

Undermining the CEO

The issue was clear. The decision had been made. Yet, that was not the end of it. It was controversial—difficult decisions often are. And controversy brings with it opinions and unwelcome gossip and speculation. Such is the nature of schools and nonprofit organizations that work with young people—who have parents!

The student was expelled for a major honor code violation. The student handbook was crystal clear regarding the violation—expulsion with no possibility to return. The administration took the appropriate steps and the student was removed from the school. Almost immediately the student's parents began to lobby for appeal and reinstatement. The parents went to the head of the school, various faculty members, even alumni to lobby on behalf of the student. On each of these occasions the individuals were informed that the administration had made a decision and the decision would not be reversed.

This went on for months. Each attempt was politely rebuffed. The parents would simply not retreat from their efforts to have their child accepted back into the school. Eventually the parents contacted the chair of the board of trustees. The head of the school was stunned to learn that the chair of the board had agreed to have lunch with the unsatisfied parents! The chair was fully aware from the very beginning of the action taken by the school. The chair was also aware of the repeated attempts on the part of the parents to have their student return to the school.

The chair of the board contacted the head of the school to inform the head that they had agreed to meet and listen to the parents on this matter. The head tried, without success, to explain to the chair that it was not appropriate to give an audience to the parents when a decision had been made months earlier. The chair angrily responded that he would have lunch with whomever he chose and that it was, in his opinion, altogether appropriate to hear them out. The head could not believe the chair had this attitude and had been so defensive. The head requested that the chair share with him the content of the conversation. The chair declined and the head never learned the outcome of their conversation. Fortunately, the chair did not make any move to have the student reinstated.

QUESTIONS FOR DISCUSSION

1. *Are there circumstances in which a student should be removed from an independent or faith-based school?*

2. *Does it appear that the school took the appropriate action? Why? Why not?*

3. *Could the school have handled the decision and aftermath differently? How?*

4. *When contacted by the parents, did the chair respond appropriately?*

5. *Briefly describe the presence or lack of presence of the following characteristics:*

   - *Collaboration:*

   - *Communication:*

   - *Trust:*

   - *Respect:*

   - *Support:*

   - *Attitude:*

6. *What could the head have done differently?*

7. *What should the chair of the board done differently?*

8. *What does this incident say about the head and the chair's relationship?*

Chapter Seven

CHARACTERISTICS AND SKILLS NECESSARY FOR SUCCESS

There is a familiar expression that applies to the manner and process of adding members to the organization's board of trustees: "If you do what you have always done, then you will get what you have always gotten." Simply stated, the board must look for other types or categories of prospective members—those who will possess the characteristics needed for the best in volunteer leadership.

7 TYPES OF BOARD MEMBERS TO CONSIDER

The committee on trustees and any others on the board who have a responsibility to secure new members of the board should consider these seven "types" of leaders:

1. Individuals who will work and accept both individual and team responsibilities.

Attracting board members to the organization is one thing; attracting individuals who will willingly accept the responsibilities of the work required in making a personal, individual commitment as well as embracing the idea that they are part of a team of trustees who must speak with one voice is quite another. This must be clearly communicated during the trustee recruiting process.

2. Well-known and respected individuals whose name, reputation, and credibility would add something to the organization.

Every person named to the board must bring something that adds value to the board and therefore to the organization. Individuals who demonstrate character and integrity and have the skills needed should always make the short list. Nonprofit organizations should look for name recognition—but not that alone. It will be difficult to attract someone simply because they are well known. Typically organizations benefit if the person is well known *and* has an interest in the organization's mission and vision.

NOTE: There are strategic ways in which the organization can identify and attract individuals who are not currently aware of what you do. One example is to establish a "board of visitors" as a way in which to engage such individuals without the responsibilities required of board members.

3. Individuals who are considered to be "on their way up" in the community but are not yet over committed.

Many communities all across the country have initiated programs that identify young leaders who are beginning to demonstrate through their success or potential an interest to give back and make a difference in their communities. One such organization is the Young Leaders Council. Their purpose is to work with young leaders (approximately twenty-five to forty years in age) and train them to understand what is involved in being an excellent board member. This is one example among many. Nonprofit organizations have a unique opportunity to attract these "up and comers" who have the potential to be outstanding board members. The downside is that they may not be in a position to make a significant financial commitment. But that ability to give may come and there are other contributions they can make immediately. This is a constituency easily overlooked. The smart organization will carefully consider opportunities to add this category of board member.

4. Well-positioned community leaders who will contribute "time, talent, and/or treasure," or leaders who will "give and get."

While this is easier for the well-known or older organization, any organization can attract these individuals to your board. First, to do so it must be a strategic priority. In other words, you must be intentional and set this as a goal for the board and be willing to be evaluated on it. Tactically, it probably starts with your current board members. Do you have someone, or more than one person, who is in such a position and has the clout and desire to assist in attracting others who fall into this category? If so, work with them to connect who they know with the organization—other board members as well as senior administrative leadership.

The whole *work, wealth, wisdom* and *time, talent, treasure* discussion regarding board responsibilities has become something of an overused cliché. But it does not make these skills any less valid or necessary. And it is certainly a starting point for a dialogue for looking at the skills needed to enhance the performance of the board.

5. Active, involved, and mature young leaders.

Maturity is a character trait often lacking. This coupled with those people who are known to be active and involved make for excellent board members. The challenge is to convince this type of individual to join your ranks. The first step is *identification*—be intentional as to whom you want. The second step is *information*—take the steps necessary to provide information that will uncover their level of interest. The third step is *involvement*—creating the opportunities to learn more about their potential interest as well as understanding of the organization's mission and vision will equip board recruiters with valuable evidence as to what kind of trustee the person is likely to become.

6. Upper-level and middle-level managers of area corporations.

All too often nonprofit organizations try to reach too high in the hierarchy of a business or corporation when seeking new board members. In fact it may not be the CEO or the president that is the best fit but rather someone in upper or middle level management. There are often very talented people at these levels who are looking for opportunities to validate their role in the company by making a commitment to a nonprofit organization in the community. They understand that giving back creates situations for moving up.

7. Active spouses, sons, and daughters of well-established leaders in the community.

This category of prospective board member should be near the top of your list to consider. Often overlooked, they have enormous potential for their own skills but also for their connections and associations with family members who are in a position to hugely impact the organization. A wealthy and influential father can be a very grateful donor when his daughter is asked to be on the board!

FOUR HELPFUL SKILLS OF BOARD MEMBERS

There are also certain skills that you should look for in prospective board members. These include:

1. Cultivate donors and solicit gifts for the organization.

As mentioned in Chapter 9, this skill is thought to be a given. Don't believe it—be very intentional regarding expectations. If this skill is a board priority then act accordingly and communicate this expectation with prospective board members as well as current ones.

2. Cultivate and recruit board members and other volunteer leaders.

It is the responsibility for good board members to seek out and find other good members to help perpetuate the work the current board is doing. An ability and willingness to understand why this is important should either be clear or made clear to the board member. The continuous flow of individuals who are prepared to serve with distinction must always be an important responsibility. It is the very fabric of what continuity is all about.

3. Understand financial position of the organization.

We all know that the board has the responsibility for the financial well-being of the organization. It is necessary and appropriate that board members grasp issues that relate to the budget, assets, endowment investment, and all matters financial. Having said that, the board and the organization is more than this. Additional perspectives are needed to provide balance. Having a core group that is well versed in the financial position is vital to sustainability.

4. Continually learn about programs of the organization.

While mission, vision, strategy, and planning are at the forefront of what the board is accountable for overseeing, they should also be informed about the programs of the organization. Much of this should jointly be accomplished through efforts of the CEO and the board chair to ensure that all board members are well acquainted with organizational objectives.

ADDITIONAL SKILLS USEFUL TO AN ORGANIZATION

In addition to the list above, these are some general skills that will always prove to be vital to the health of any organization:

1. Ability to listen, analyze, and think clearly and creatively.

Listening skills are often overlooked but badly needed. Part of effective listening skills is the recognition of the idea that "it's not all about me." This is a valuable perspective, and it suggests an attitude of teamwork, collaboration, and trust.

2. Ability to work with people individually and in groups.

Working well with others includes the ability to work together for common goals, to work as a team, find consensus, and when appropriate, compromise.

3. Willingness to prepare for and participate in committee meetings.

Service on the board clearly means active involvement and participation. Showing up for board meetings is merely the first step. Engaging in the real work requires serving on one or more committees.

4. Contribute personal resources in a generous way suggesting board membership is a philanthropic priority during the time of active involvement and service.

Giving as generously as one is able suggests that during the time on the board the organization is unquestionably a philanthropic priority. There should be a distinction someone makes between serving on an organization's board and being a constituent. Take, for example, your alma mater. As an alumnus or alumna of a school, you may be a donor depending on numerous factors, chief among them the experience you had as a student and the impact the school has had on your life and career. When you agree to serve as a trustee of that school, your relationship changes dramatically and the school becomes more central to your volunteer commitments. Your giving should therefore align with your commitment and thus become a financial priority to the best of your capacity.

5. Opening doors in the community is beneficial to the organization.

Utilizing your sphere of influence, it is incumbent to provide introductions and access where it will have the most impact. Part of why someone is asked to serve on the board is for this very reason.

CASE STUDY #6

An Encouraging Sign

In a visit with a head of school we began a conversation about governance. I was sharing with my new friend the work that I was doing in the area of governance. He had been the head of this school for four years so I asked him if he was still working for/with the board chair when he was appointed or if there had been a transition to someone new in that role.

One of the most critical issues for a school, or any nonprofit organization, is the ability to successfully navigate the transition from the chair in place when a new head of school is appointed to a new chair. I address this issue with some directness in *The Board Game* because this is a place ripe for a breakdown in the relationship between the head (or CEO), board, and board chair.

His answer was yes, that a new chair of the board had been appointed. Our ensuing discussion gave me hope because he described almost the ideal scenario about how this transition can most effectively occur. When this happens the school and ultimately the students, parents, alumni, faculty, staff, *and* board members will benefit from the positive environment that will result.

He shared with me that when it was time to appoint a new chair, he, the head of school, was not only included in the discussion about who should be the next chair, he was given the opportunity to express any concerns regarding anyone being considered. In addition, he was given veto power over anyone he deemed unqualified for the position. During the course of our conversation he revealed that he had expressed serious concerns with two of the prospective candidates because he possessed knowledge that could have blossomed into a major problem.

There are seven essential characteristics that must be in place for the head (or nonprofit CEO) and board chair to work effectively. This remarkable episode suggests the presence of all seven:

1. *Communication and Collaboration.* The ability to candidly discuss the needs of the organization (school) in such a way that demonstrates a desire to do what is right and what is best takes precedence.

2. *Respect.* Mutual respect must be present to create an environment in which all relevant issues can be put forward.

3. *Trust.* Trust is necessary to confidentially debate strengths and weaknesses of those being considered.

4. *Support.* The ability to support the decision of the head is critical to enhancing the relationship.

5. *Shared Vision.* Leadership is the key to every aspect of the organization and agreeing on the kind of individual to move forward is essential.

6. *Attitude.* The attitude of everyone involved suggests the positive way in which to approach such a critical decision.

7. *Leadership.* Everything rises and falls with leadership. Select the right person and all things are possible. The wrong decision and the wrong leader could have dire consequences for the school or organization.

Congratulations to this head of school and to his enlightened board who clearly grasp the importance of what a genuine difference leadership can make. His story encourages me to believe that such relationships can thrive.

QUESTIONS FOR DISCUSSION

1. *Why do you believe this relationship works?*

2. *What should your bylaws say about board chair succession?*

3. *What advice would you give other nonprofit organizations about this issue?*

4. *Would different individuals in these roles produce different results?*

5. *Why does succession in leadership matter?*

Chapter Eight

STRUCTURING THE BOARD FOR SUCCESS

There are numerous ways for the board to be structured. Many of these unique ways in which the board fulfills its obligation can be found in the language in the bylaws and policies adopted by the board. What are best practices and what structure results in a significant group of individuals working together to achieve greatness for the organization?

BOARD MANUAL

The board manual is one of the most useful resources to assist in providing a sense of integration and belonging to individual members of the board. It is important that this document be attractively presented in a loose-leaf notebook binder that is given to each new board member and updated during their time of service on the board of trustees. While a board notebook may seem like "old school," there should be a "place" where such information can succinctly tell the story of the organization and provide board members with an overview and outline of the organization.

Board manuals should include the following information:

- Organization's charter

- Bylaws

- Description and brief history of the organization

- Schedule of the plan of work for the board

- Roster of board members, officers, committee make-up, and past chairs

- Statement of policies

- Organizational chart

- Current budget

- Copies of publications—magazines, brochures, marketing and development materials

It is important that the manual be prepared by a collaboration of the committee on trustees, the organization's CEO, and other staff leaders. Each time new trustees are added the board manual should be updated. Updates must also be distributed to the entire board.

BYLAWS AND COMMITTEE DESCRIPTIONS

As a 501(c)(3) organization, bylaws are required as documents legally and fundamentally necessary to be a nonprofit organization. Bylaws document how the organization is governed. Bylaws may be very detailed or may be very broadly defined. Each organization will determine for themselves exactly what is included and what is excluded from this document. While bylaws constitute the governing rules of the organization that should not imply that they have to be lengthy and contain more legal jargon than is absolutely necessary. For a more complete look at bylaws and their place in your organization, please see Appendixes A, B, and C.

Whether in the bylaws or in some other document of the nonprofit organization, having written descriptions of the responsibilities of each of the standing committees is a very good thing. There are several reasons why this is a good idea including:

1. Written committee description demonstrates the organization's commitment to providing resources and information that will help trustees understand and perform their duties.

2. Written descriptions leave minimal room for misinterpretation as to priorities and needs.

3. Written descriptions help prospective and new trustees move promptly to learning about the organization and the committee structure.

THE APPROPRIATE SIZE OF THE BOARD

The number of members on the board of trustees has much to

do with the history and institutional culture of the organization. Most boards have evolved over time to reflect the current nature of the organization. It is probably true with many organizations that they looked at similar organizations to help determine the number of board members. Ultimately the issue of size must be the decision of the board itself. Again, collaboration with CEO and staff leadership is a key in reviewing these issues.

Problems will certainly surface if the board becomes too large or too small. When a board becomes too large it often creates an "inner" board. This inner board may be formalized like the executive committee, or may be a less structured group that becomes a functioning center of control.

The board must be large enough to carry out their necessary duties and responsibilities. A board that is too small in number will not be able to carry out the necessary policy guidance and leadership that is vital to the organization's ability to carry out its mission and vision. If too small it may not be able to accommodate all groups or constituencies that should be represented for decision making. A small board may also become too closely knit and clannish. And there may be the practical challenge of not having enough to constitute a quorum.

There are several different ways to determine the appropriate size of the board. One is more objective, calculating the number of committees, the number of members per committee, the number of officers, and consideration for those who will serve on special or ad hoc committees.

It is best for boards to have an uneven number of voting members. While many operate and make most decisions by consensus, there is always the very real possibility of a tie vote on certain issues. If the board does have an even number of members then provision must be made as to how a tie vote will be broken. While boards rarely find themselves in this predicament, it is wise to be aware of the potential problems that could arise.

TENURE

How long someone stays on the board is a matter of interest and concern for all of the board members. There are various discussions and debates that argue for, on the one hand, a prolonged tenure. And there are those who argue for a more brief time of service. The weight, however, suggests that neither extreme constitutes a best practice. The term of service must be long enough to provide all-important continuity of policies and practice, but short enough to secure and ensure continuous freshness of perspective.

There are two resolutions that address this issue. First is the establishment of definite terms of appointment. The second is the limitation of the number of consecutive terms each member may serve. Although these two resolutions are related, they are distinctive.

The argument of no term limits dismisses the larger issue of having fresh perspective and provides more people with the opportunity to be involved and contribute in different ways with the organization.

Many organizations have adopted the three-year term of membership with the opportunity to serve a second term, for a total of six years of service. After that, many bylaws state that the person must go off the board for at least one year before being considered again.

OVERLAPPING TERMS

Most boards have defined terms for their members with provision for overlapping membership. These defined term limits provide:

- A pattern of beginning and termination points that allows for continuity and for changes in membership.

- Built-in motivation for those who want to continue on the board.

- An easier plan to build a broader base of support.

- A consistent mechanism for removing uninterested, ineffective members from the board.

For example, if a board of an organization had eighteen members, with three-year term limits, then a typical "class" would include six each year—with some returning for a second term and some beginning a first term.

LIMITATION OF TERMS

While it is not universally advisable for volunteer boards to have term limitations, for most boards some kind of term limitation should be seriously considered. The concept is a simple one—every member of the board should be required to go off the board after serving a consecutive number of terms, usually two or three terms. As stated above, many bylaws written today state that after a set number of terms the board member may not be considered again until the individual has been off the board for not less than one year. Even a particularly valuable board member should step down for some period before being elected again.

PAST BOARD MEMBERS

The question almost never fails to arise, what is the most useful way to engage past board members? Many organizations do not have a very good answer to this question as they simply allow them to fade into the past. However, there are organizations that recognize the value and importance of these people and develop very clever ways to encourage their continual engagement. Some of these ways are more formal than others. The creation of a structure such as a board of advisors can be made up exclusively or partly with past board members. Regardless of the manner in which this happens, it is in the organization's best interest to keep these past board members involved and engaged.

SELECTION AND TRANSITION
OF THE BOARD CHAIR

The chair of the board is an enormously important position in the organization. That person's relationship with the entire board and the CEO (executive director) of the organization is critical to living out the mission. No other relationship is as critical as that of the board chair and CEO. Through the bylaws and the culture of the board, the chair must be carefully selected to ensure that it is someone who possesses qualities of leadership, integrity, responsibility, respect, and support. It is imperative that the chair be an individual who understands the role of the board and is not troubled by the need to restrain and, if necessary, discipline members of the board if they fail to adhere to policies and guidelines.

Another critical component is the manner in which the transition occurs between one board chair and the next. This task should be articulated in the organization's bylaws and implemented in the most seamless way possible. The board should avoid extremes in personality and working relationships when choosing the board chair. Working with the board and CEO should be viewed as a primary responsibility of the chair.

COMMITTEE STRUCTURE

Of all the aspects of board membership it is the committee structure and process that is most subject to mock horror and heavy-handed humor. In spite of the humor and misconceptions, committees continue to flourish and be an integral part of the volunteer board structure.

There are at least three types of committees—standing; special (or ad hoc); and coordinating.

1. *Standing committees* are those that remain in existence indefinitely in order to consider ongoing issues of the board. Such committees are identified in the bylaws and are often accompanied by a description of the committee responsibilities. These typically include a budget (or finance) committee, committee on trustees (or nominating committee), building/grounds committee, and development committee. Organizations may also include other standing committees.

2. *Special* or *ad hoc committees* are appointed to address a specific situation and then cease to exist

once the issue has been resolved. An example might be a search committee that is created to conduct a search for a position within the organization. Once the position is filled the need for the committee goes out of existence.

3. *Coordinating committees* are ones that provide general direction and guidance. An example would be the executive committee. This committee typically includes the officers of the board and may include committee chairs and perhaps other board members.

As stated earlier, committee functions should be clearly stated and, if a standing committee, be defined in the organization's bylaws. Minutes from board meetings should indicate when special committees are established.

In many cases board members have an opportunity to indicate their committee preferences when they come onto a board. The board chair usually appoints committee members and often, but not always, attempts to follow the wishes of the board member.

Such appointments typically are with the input of the committee chair as well as the organization's CEO. As provided in many bylaws, the chair and the CEO are *ex officio* members of each committee and serve without vote.

Committee appointment is one of the most important responsibilities of the chair. Competence, interest, expertise, skills, and, above all, what is best for the organization are key factors in making these appointments.

COMMITTEE MEMBERS OUTSIDE
OF THE BOARD

It is not uncommon for many organizations to have committees that include both board and non-board members. These non-board committee members may provide a certain knowledge or expertise in a particular area. Depending on the person's interest level, the board may decide to ask the non-board member to consider joining the board.

Non-board members who serve on board committees rarely serve as the committee's chair. There are certain exceptions to this practice, but they are not the norm.

Chapter Nine

BOARDS AND FUNDRAISING: MAKING A STATEMENT ABOUT COMMITMENT

Perhaps the task of a nonprofit board that is most often misunderstood or neglected during the recruitment process is that of fundraising on behalf of the organization. Often these issues reveal the need for better ongoing communication about expectations.

UNDERSTANDING FUNDRAISING PRINCIPLES

What is needed is a candid dialogue so that there is no misunderstanding when the time comes for the board individually and collectively to give. If this expectation is not made clear then don't be surprised when there is some resentment to the request.

It is imperative that board members understand and embrace fundraising principles. Philanthropy has numerous aspects and some of the basic ones include:

People make gifts because they want to do so.

People don't give because they are forced to make a gift. Reflect for a moment on your own giving patterns. There are often several motivating factors in your decision to make a contribution. Ultimately you give because you have a desire to, you care deeply about the organization and its mission, and because you want to make a difference.

People make gifts to make a change for the good.

The organization must demonstrate *why* it is important for people to give. It must be explained that the gift can be responsible for the good the organization is doing. People won't give simply because you have been in existence for a long time. They won't give because of a compelling story or mission. Much more is necessary. In seeking gifts, your strategy should embrace that reality and motivation on the part of donors.

People give to opportunities, not needs.

More often than not, people respond to a compelling vision, not to the organization's budgetary needs. People want to give because they have been presented with an opportunity to achieve something special and meaningful, not because the organization "needs the money." It is completely inadequate to say you need money. A compelling vision that demonstrates the impact of the organization—that is what will win the day.

People give to success, not distress.

Donors want to believe that their support is going to further the mission of a successful, thriving organization. Organizations that struggle with leadership, mission, or finances have a much more difficult time convincing prospective donors of their viability and whether or not they can achieve what they say they can.

THE BOARD'S RESPONSIBILITY FOR FUNDRAISING

Almost every description you will find of the board of trustees will include statements regarding fundraising. As a 501(c)(3) nonprofit organization, the board of trustees has a clearly defined fiduciary responsibility meaning that the financial health of the organization falls within their responsibilities. As a result, some boards will no doubt see that part of the financial health revolves around contributing financial resources to ensure the organization's health and sustainability.

It is practically a universal truth in fundraising that donors to an organization will take their cue from the board as to how generous they will be, or whether they will give at all. The principle behind this statement directly addresses the issue that those closest to understanding and embracing the organization's mission are mostly likely the ones providing significant support. It follows then that if these people don't support the organization, why should anyone else? In other words, if you can't get the board to give, how are you going to convince anyone else to give? It is not only a fair question; it is the question that must be addressed before any other.

There are those boards that believe that fundraising can be delegated to the organization's CEO/executive director and development staff (if the organization has made this much-needed investment). While delegating certain functions is very appropriate, it should not be assumed that they are now somehow exempt from any further involvement.

Some organizations have established foundations for the purpose of raising funds. Many public universities, public libraries, and public schools, for example, have created foundations for the purpose of raising funds on behalf of the organization they serve. These foundations may also have their own board. However, the board of the "parent" organization should still maintain involvement and support for fundraising.

POSITIONING THE BOARD TO BE SUCCESSFUL

For the board of trustees to understand and embrace their responsibilities in giving and participating in the different aspects of the fundraising process, it is imperative that they be encouraged to participate in training and educational opportunities that will increase their knowledge and understanding of how they can make the greatest impact possible in this area. This includes leadership from the CEO, the chief development officer, the development committee, and chair. Communicating the value of participating in such events elevates this issue to an entirely different level.

WAYS TO HELP WITHOUT ASKING FOR MONEY

How often has it been said, "I'll do anything but fundraising!" People will attempt all kinds of dangerous stunts but ask them to solicit a gift and they break out in a sweat. Fundraising is much more than "asking" for a gift. There is a process and board members have numerous opportunities to assist with this other than asking for a gift.

Contributing

This should be the first step for every board member. Every board member should contribute as generously as they are able—recognizing that giving should be a priority during the time of service on the board. The board must be 100 percent in financial support before going to others to ask for support.

Formulating the Plans, Programs, Mission, and Case

Each of these is vital to the effectiveness of the organization and represent an important responsibility of the board. The plans, programs, mission, and case are each and all supported by a viable fundraising program. Board members on the development committee, or elsewhere on the board, can provide meaningful leadership to ensure that each of these activities is achieved.

Building the List of Prospective Donors

The organization may rely heavily on the need to ever expand its base of support. A fundamental way this happens is for individuals who care deeply about the organization are in an ideal position to identify individuals, foundations, and corporations who have similar interests. Board members have a "sphere of influence" that can be accessed to gain support for the organization. It is imperative that they be approached about how best to accomplish this.

Assisting in the Research and Evaluation of Prospects

Never underestimate the importance and value of research on prospects and the preparation needed before a major gift visit is made. Board members may be in a position to provide helpful information that impacts the amount and manner in which the prospective donor is approached.

Cultivating Prospects

People are more likely to give when they have a relationship with individuals who are a part of the organization. It is hard to beat the personal touch. Cultivating prospects by providing information and insight about the mission and vision of the organization can be a very successful strategy in bringing in more donors.

Making Introductions

Making the most of connections board members have, they can introduce others to those they do not feel comfortable soliciting. Smoothing the way for someone else to solicit can go far in securing that gift. Networking is a vital piece of the fundraising picture. Board members have great connections and these connections should be put to work on behalf of the organization.

Helping and Supporting Fundraising Events

Events are a time-consuming enterprise for even the best of organizations. Board members can play an essential role supporting these events by serving on the committee(s) charged with holding the event. Depending on the complexity and ambition of the event, there may well be numerous ways for board members to be supportive.

Assisting in Getting Out Annual Fund Appeal Letters

Sending out annual fund appeal letters is one of those traditions that still linger in this age of online communication. If your organization sends out these letters, why not add something special to the appeal—a note from the board chair or any member of the board? It is an appropriate way to stay connected to prospective or existing donors but does not step over the line into operational matters.

Writing Thank You Notes

Even in an age of texting and e-mails, nothing trumps a handwritten note of thanks for someone's generosity. This is genuine stewardship—taking the time to say "thank you" in a way rarely seen today. Board members can support this effort—especially when the member has been involved with identifying the donor and/or soliciting the gift.

MOTIVATING AND INSPIRING OTHERS

Motivation, inspiration, encouragement, and communication all play a significant role in leadership. It is important that board members motivate one another and hold one another accountable for the success of the organization. What is it that will motivate a board member to become involved? A general appeal at a board meeting is not nearly as effective as a direct, personal appeal from the board chair. Think about that when you are considering how to get someone to do something that needs to be done.

One of the biggest challenges in working with and motivating board members is to get them to do *what* they say they will do, *when* they say they will do it! Successful and inspired boards have this challenge figured out.

In the end, there are four primary areas where board members struggle with fundraising:

1. Board members often do not understand philanthropic giving and asking. They fail to recognize that people want to give and take great joy in doing so.

2. Board members are reluctant to accept the fact that part of what comes with being a board is fundraising. Rare is the nonprofit organization that does not have a need to raise funds and rare is the board that escapes this responsibility.

3. Board members do not grasp the concept that there are many ways to be involved in the fundraising process without directly soliciting a gift. There is magic in the process and often board members can assist in securing the gift without asking for the gift.

4. Board members are slow to realize the most effective way to motivate and encourage members to act is to personally ask that they accept specific assignments—including the encouragement to support fundraising efforts.

Chapter Ten

EXECUTIVE SESSIONS: WHERE BOARDS GO WRONG

A nonprofit leader shared the disturbing and unfortunate news that the board of trustees of the organization had decided to start having executive sessions. Such sessions are usually held after the conclusion of business from the regular board meeting. Excluded from the session are staff and ex-officio members of the board—including the CEO or the head of school for an independent school. I am philosophically very opposed to these sessions. During my career I have been a nonprofit CEO as well as board member for several different organizations. So I recognize the perspective of both. Executive sessions are destructive and will inevitably lead to an atmosphere of distrust. They are a distraction and may lead to the departure of the CEO.

The first question I had is, why? Why would the board decide to do this? Especially given that the CEO was very successful and the board had never held executive sessions before. He indicated a new board chair had just begun his duties and wanted to include executive sessions. I then asked, was the new chair sharing information discussed during the sessions with the CEO? The answer was no—no information was being shared. I would not wish to be that CEO.

As I reflected on this new situation I thought it would be timely to clarify why executive sessions are not healthy for the organization. Here are the top five reasons why I believe executive sessions are damaging.

1. Executive sessions create a climate of mistrust between the CEO and the governing board.

One of the most important characteristics that must be present for organizational effectiveness is for the board chair and the CEO to trust one another, to respect the role that each must play. Executive sessions do not produce trust or respect.

2. Executive sessions demonstrate that a true partnership is absent from the relationship.

Working together means just that. The CEO and board chair have different responsibilities, but they must work together to achieve mission and vision for the organization.

3. Executive sessions may suggest that the board has something to hide.

If they do not have something to hide, why hold these sessions? What is it that the board can't share with the CEO? Other than issues of evaluation and compensation there is no reason to keep anything from the CEO.

4. Executive sessions demonstrate a lack of understanding of the board's role.

All too often executive sessions are forums to spread gossip and discuss staff or other matters in unproductive and inappropriate ways.

5. Executive sessions often include discussions about issues with which they have limited or no information.

Meeting in the absence of the CEO, the board may lack the information needed to effectively discuss the matter.

There will be those who believe differently. They will argue that executive sessions are harmless and that thinking otherwise is simply being paranoid. Some claim executive sessions are fine and should be a part of every meeting agenda. I respectfully disagree and further, of the boards I have served on and been familiar with, none include an executive session as part of the regular agenda. Does the board have a right and responsibility to discuss the performance of the CEO? Absolutely! How this is done is the key. Does the board have the right to discuss other issues in the absence of the CEO (often an ex-officio member of the board)? I argue that not if they wish to have a collaborative, trusting relationship with the CEO.

Is it possible that something constructive can result from these sessions? Yes, but why exclude the CEO when this individual can add to any conversation the board is having? Nonprofit organizations and their boards should strive for more, to be better than this. They should be seeking to be the best possible.

Leadership is recognized in people of courage—individuals who inspire, motivate, and encourage. These are the kind of board members who will not make the mistake of equating executive sessions with doing the real work of the organization. This is the kind of organization that should be supported.

What's Support Got to Do with It?

There it was—on the table almost as soon as the words came out of Jeff's mouth. Jeff was facilitating a retreat for the board. He was discussing the most important responsibilities of the board and he was describing the incredibly important truism that the best, most successful organizations are those in which the relationship between the CEO, the board chair, and entire governing body must be based on trust and support. The facts were these: twenty-one members on the board; met five times a year; seven standing committees.

The retreat was focused on best practices for governance and the commencement of a strategic planning process that was to include a comprehensive assessment of all aspects of the organization—including governance responsibilities. Jeff was in the process of sharing board responsibilities. Specifically he was addressing the issue of the critical nature of the relationship between the CEO and board chair—the fact that this partnership set the tone for so much of what could be accomplished.

Jeff believed one of the very best examples for communicating this partnership was to state with candor and clarity why holding executive sessions—discussions by the board without the presence of the CEO—were a very bad idea and how such sessions resulted in distrust, suspicion, and a failure to provide support for the CEO. It was at this moment that the new chair of the board spoke up and expressed his opinion on this topic. "I see nothing wrong with having executive sessions. As long as the CEO and I have a relationship based on trust then I fail to see the harm in having an occasional executive session."

In Jeff's earlier comments he described the circumstances when having an executive session was appropriate, indeed necessary. This, he said, would be needed when the CEO was being evaluated and when their compensation package was being considered. Other than that, Jeff made it clear there really was no other reason to exclude the CEO. You were either partners or not. Following the board chair's comment Jeff responded, "If your relationship is based on trust, then why do you not trust the CEO enough to include her in any conversation with the board?" The chair countered, "She knows that I support her in every way." Jeff responded, "What's support got do with it? If you don't demonstrate trust then support seems to be just talk without conviction."

The board chair paused a moment and admitted that perhaps he would need to reflect on this and rethink his position on executive sessions. Jeff thought this was a positive step on the board understanding that they had a wide range of strategic challenges to address but having executive sessions could be eliminated from the list.

QUESTIONS FOR DISCUSSION

1. *What does this story tell you about the new board chair understanding his responsibilities?*

2. *Why is trust critical to the relationship between CEO and board chair?*

3. *Under what circumstances would this relationship be tested?*

4. *Support is such an important character trait the board chair must demonstrate at every opportunity. Reflecting on your own circumstances, can you cite examples of situations in which the board chair supported or backed you up when a difficult or con-troversial issue surfaced?*

Chapter Eleven

BOARD EVALUATION: KEY COMPONENTS TO SUSTAINING EXCELLENCE

As stated elsewhere, a board's ability to meaningfully evaluate their work and impact on the organization is somewhat suspect. Some boards do it well; other boards, not so much. The most useful way to sustain excellence is to identify the key areas of self-evaluation to create the framework to provide the data and information necessary.

The different categories suggest those areas of work on which the board should be focused. Viewed as a questionnaire, these seven different categories and questions should be answered with a "yes, we are doing this" or "no, we're not doing this." If the answer is "no," then the organization must assign responsibility to ensure that the question can eventually be answered "yes." You'll find these questions listed again in Appendix I with room for your responses.

These key areas include:

- Planning
- Selection and Composition
- Organization
- Orientation and Training
- Meetings
- Individual Trustees (experienced and new)
- CEO/Executive Director/Head of School

PLANNING

The board should, almost above any other factor, be a group that devotes significant time to planning. The central questions in this area should include:

1. Is there a clear, succinct mission statement that is not only current but also understood by all trustees?

2. Is there a strategic plan and is there a process in place for periodic review of the plan?

3. Have all facets of the organization been considered when formulating the plan?

4. Do "action items" include a funding mechanism? Is there a way to fund the vision?

5. Does the board establish annual goals for itself?

6. Do board members participate in professional development opportunities?

SELECTION AND COMPOSITION

As discussed throughout, there is nothing more critical to the success of an organization than the processes in place for the selection and composition of the board. In this category, the key questions include:

1. What is the structure of the committee on trustees?

2. Is the committee active and engaged with all board members?

3. Does the committee have a matrix of prospective board members that identifies skills needed—both short-term and long-term?

4. Is the size of the board a positive or a negative?

5. Are all committees functioning and effective?

6. Are the CEO and board chair included as ex-officio members of the committee?

ORGANIZATION

How the board is organized reflects effectiveness in meeting the goals and objectives of the organization. The key questions include:

1. Are the bylaws clear, concise, up-to-date, and followed?

2. Is the committee structure of the board valuable in meeting the demands of the board and the needs of the organization?

3. Does the board seek ways to involve all constituencies of the organization?

4. Does the board recognize and act on the difference between their responsibilities and those of the organization's administration?

5. Overall, does the board understand its responsibilities?

6. Are there individual trustees who are not effective in their role?

7. Does the board review its work and is this process meaningful?

ORIENTATION AND TRAINING

You hope that the committee on trustees has done an outstanding job in identifying and selecting trustees. Even so, there is more that must be done. Orientation as well as ongoing training and education will encourage trustees to focus on being the best they can be. The key questions in this category include:

1. Is there a formal orientation session for all new trustees?

2. Is there a board policy manual and does it include information useful to becoming familiar with the work of the board and the organization?

3. Does the policy manual include a clear definition of conflict of interest and how the board addresses this issue?

4. Is there a structured, formalized program for board education?

5. Is funding available for board members to attend/ participate in professional development opportunities designed for the board?

6. Does the board conduct an annual or periodic retreat as a way to explore a range of issues beneficial to both the board and the organization?

MEETINGS

The issues surrounding meetings are more complex than perhaps initially believed. Meetings set the tone for a "board culture" that in many ways defines who they are, how they operate, and the impact they have. Questions regarding such issues as frequency and length should not be taken lightly and include:

1. Is the current number of meetings per year about right? Are more needed and why? Are fewer needed and why?

2. Do board meetings typically last longer than two hours?

3. Is the agenda properly prepared and reviewed by the officers or executive committee prior to the meeting?

4. Is the agenda and supporting documentation sent to board members prior to the board meeting?

5. Do committees meet at intervals between board meetings?

6. Is the staff liaison role understood and respected by board committees?

7. Are committee reports effective and useful?

8. Is financial information presented and conveyed in a manner that non-financial people can easily understand?

INDIVIDUAL TRUSTEES

Each individual trustee plays a significant role as a part of the board of trustees. The board is no better than its worst trustee. Therefore, because each trustee is a key member of the board, the manner in which each trustee does their job is essential. The key questions for the specific trustee are:

1. Is the board member prepared for both committee and board meetings?

2. Does each member capably perform assigned as well as volunteered responsibilities?

3. Does the board member recommend others to serve on the board?

4. Does the board member give as generously as possible?

5. Does the board member recommend donors and solicit support?

6. Does the board member respect the work of the entire board?

7. Does the board member fully embrace and defend issues such as confidentiality and conflict of interest?

CEO/EXECUTIVE DIRECTOR

The relationship between the CEO, the board chair, and the entire governing board is critical to the health and sustainability of the organization. The key questions that support this relationship include:

1. Does the board support the CEO and view his or her role as one of partnership and collaboration?

2. Does the CEO establish annual goals and set goals that reflect the mission and vision of the organization?

3. Does the board have in place a fair and helpful way to evaluate the work of the CEO?

4. Is the evaluation presented in a way that demonstrates respect for the work performed by the CEO and the staff?

5. Does the board provide in the budget continuing education and professional development opportunities for the CEO?

- - -

Boards that do the best job of evaluating their own work are boards that embrace this as a key to being the best board possible. In such cases the organization thrives because the vision shared by the key constituencies will result in a dynamic, thriving, vigorous, *and* sustainable organization!

CASE STUDY #8

The Challenge of Communication

The question was a good one—it was raised to get a sense of what worked best. There was no hidden agenda and no thought given to hijack the issue. As the chair of the board, Steven was well within his authority to seek the opinion on the matter from his new but very experienced CEO. Was there a way to determine board value and success as that issue relates to the number of meetings held each year? What was the specific relevance about meeting bi-monthly, quarterly or on a different schedule?

It was a question raised during the search process. At the time Sharon, then a candidate for the position, had responded by indicating what her current organization's practice was. She made two things very clear to Steven. First, she believed that quarterly meetings were the best practice because that schedule allowed the standing committees to function by holding meetings at least once between each of the quarterly board meetings. Second, quarterly board meetings meant that the organization's staff had time to prepare for these meetings and the committee meetings but did not place an undue burden of always preparing for board and committee meetings. Sharon felt very strongly that this model was efficient and meaningful and fostered the best possible relationship between the board and staff.

The Challenge of Communication

Steven stated that the organization, for the past several years, had been meeting bi-monthly. This every-other-month schedule seemed to be working and most of the board members seemed to be content with this schedule. He admitted that it did make scheduling committee meetings around board meetings a bit of a challenge. Sharon replied that while she preferred the quarterly meeting schedule she would be fine and glad to adjust to bi-monthly meetings should she be the successful candidate.

A few weeks later Steven called to inform Sharon that she had been selected as the executive director. She was thrilled and they discussed various employment details. Over the next few weeks they talked several times over a variety of issues. Eventually the conversation came back around to the number of board meetings the organization would have per year. Steven informed Sharon that the decision had been made to change to quarterly meetings. Naturally, she assumed that Steven had discussed this with the full board and that either by vote or consensus the board had agreed with Steven's recommendation to switch to quarterly board meetings.

After Sharon had moved to the community where the organization was located she and Steven began to prepare for the first meeting. In preparation she initiated meetings with individual board members—typically over lunch or coffee. During some of these conversations she began to sense that the issue of the number of board meetings was not universally embraced or understood. She also sensed some resentment of Steven for the manner in which this decision had been made. Apparently at a board meeting prior to Sharon's arrival Steven announced that beginning after her arrival the board would switch from bi-monthly to quarterly meetings. Further, his announcement strongly hinted that this change was highly recommended by Sharon—almost sounding as if it were a condition of employment. Sharon was stunned.

Soon after that she scheduled a meeting with Steven to find out exactly what the story was. She made sure he understood that their earlier conversation was just a dialogue about possibilities. While she favored quarterly meetings, she would be fine with bi-monthly meeting until such time as the issue could have proper review. Steven dismissed her concerns and in effect said that as the chair of the board it was his prerogative to make these types of decisions. She wanted to say something about consensus and team building but decided it would not be prudent to do so. She also wanted him to know that she was being partly blamed for the decision and just as she was getting to know the trustees this issue had put something of a dark cloud over her. Sharon was troubled that there was a very definite communication challenge that needed addressing.

QUESTIONS FOR DISCUSSION

1. What does this encounter tell you about Steven and Sharon's relationship?

2. What does this encounter reveal about Steven's relationship with the board?

3. What is your opinion of Sharon's case for quarterly board meetings?

4. What factors or circumstances should be considered when deciding how many meetings is the right number?

5. Is there a correlation between the number of board

meetings and the board doing the best possible job of governing the organization?

6. What does this situation say about Steven's leadership style?

7. How do you believe board members should have reacted to the way in which this was communicated?

8. Do you believe this type of change should result in a change in the bylaws?

9. What does this story say regarding collaboration and trust?

10. How should this matter have been resolved?

Chapter Twelve

THE GOVERNANCE PROMISE

In my book *The Board Game*, I devote a chapter to a concept I created called The Governance Promise. It is such a valuable concept and way in which the board should view its work and its relationship with the organization that I felt it should be included in this book as well.

The Governance Promise is comprised of six statements that speak directly to attitude, behavior, and reflection about the work of the board. The idea is not revolutionary but articulating it in this way reflects a shift in the way to address the fundamental work of the organization and the most meaningful way to live out its mission and vision. It is the capstone covenant that defines the board of trustees.

Promise One

As a trustee, I promise to uphold an environment where trust and respect are exhibited and adopted as the only way in which all business between the leadership of the organization and the governing board is carried out.

Promise Two

As a trustee, I promise to maintain a distinctive, positive experience in which the organization thrives because of the partnership established between the leadership of the organization and the governing board.

Promise Three

As a trustee, I promise to foster a welcoming spirit of cooperation in which the needs of and priorities of the organization will always prevail over my agenda or self-interest.

Promise Four

As a trustee, I promise that even under circumstances in which the organization is under pressure to depart from its mission and goals, the relationship I have with the staff and governing board will hold fast and work through whatever conflict or crisis exists.

Promise Five

As a trustee, I promise to support a culture in which transitions, such as those created when a new board chair is appointed, are seamless and come with little interruption to the CEO or the trustees.

Promise Six

As a trustee, I promise to make a commitment to being a model organization, reaching for the highest standards of innovation, professionalism, and excellence.

This is what being a trustee should be about. Having these statements as the standard and on which the work of a trustee is based has the potential to revolutionize nonprofit organizations and establish inspired governing boards.

CASE STUDY #9

An Evaluation Gone Wrong

Greg was well into his third year as the executive director of a well-known and well-established nonprofit organization. His evaluation the first two years had been overwhelmingly positive. As a result, he received the maximum bonus provided for in his contract. He had been evaluated on agreed upon criteria established by the committee on the executive director that included the current board chair, the immediate past board chair, and the vice-chair of the board. Most of the criteria centered on meeting budgetary numbers in terms of overall revenue, fundraising, and expense control. There were other factors but the biggest concern was meeting the budget as the budget included programs and services the organization provided.

The third year was different. An individual had risen through the ranks for the board that was both vice-chair and treasurer—an anomaly in the bylaws Greg viewed with suspicion. In the spring of Greg's third year he met with Brenda, the board chair, and Paul, the vice-chair and treasurer. Over lunch the three discussed a variety of issues and finally Paul launched into what his agenda really was. He began by saying he did not like the way the last two evaluations had been conducted and he was determined to do things differently this time. He shared with Greg an evaluation survey he was planning to provide all trustees. Greg was a little surprised because no survey had been used before. But he indicated he had no problem with the trustees completing the survey. Greg was confident that the results would be favorable.

In Paul's next breath he stated that he was going to have Greg's leadership team also complete the survey. Greg looked at both Paul and Brenda, stunned by what he had just heard. He made it immediately clear he had concerns about this. He was a leader with high expectations that sometimes led to disagreements with some of the decisions that were made. He also knew his number one priority was to do what was best for the organization, not to try to win a popularity contest. Furthermore, these staff members reported to and worked with Greg—not with Paul and Brenda.

Greg made it clear he was concerned about having these senior administrators take the survey. Paul was direct in saying he was unconcerned with what Greg thought and was planning to meet with these staff members and provide them with the survey.

Three weeks later Greg was asked to resign by Paul and Brenda. The decision was based in large part by what the staff had said. Greg was speechless. In less than a year he had gone from an evaluation in which he was praised for his vision, numerous accomplishments, and a genuine sense that the organization was making huge strides...to a shameful and despicable ending to his tenure. Yes, Greg realized that some decisions were not popular and knew that the senior staff was not always in agreement. However, Greg always asked for and received their input, always listened to their perspective, and always respected their recommendations. In the end Paul had found a way to bring down Greg and get someone into the position who would do his bidding.

QUESTIONS FOR DISCUSSION

1. What is your opinion of Paul's methods?

2. Do you believe it is a best practice for an officer on a board of trustees to hold more than one office at a time?

3. Should the staff have been surveyed?

4. Why do you believe Brenda (the board chair) was not more vocal?

5. What do you believe motivated Paul?

6. What criteria do you believe should be measured as a part of Greg's evaluation?

7. What lessons would be most beneficial for Greg to learn?

Chapter Thirteen

THE COVENANT AGREEMENT

The boards of nonprofit 501(c)(3) organizations have a legal as well as fiduciary responsibility to ensure that the organizations thrive by living out their mission and vision. These boards take their role seriously and are capable of providing a great service to the organizations they lead. While we all strive for the ideal, to have the possibility of working alongside individuals who want to lead by serving, who possess great attitude and skills, and who want to work in partnership with the organization's leadership creates a very special environment.

How can you ensure that the board will embrace these issues and accept them as the way in which the fabric of board work will occur? Do you rely on a verbal understanding? Are the bylaws crafted in such a way as to speak to issues such as these? What document, if any, does the board sign signaling their belief, understanding, and support? The vast majority of organizations do not have a formal, documented understanding that articulates the focus of board responsibilities. Why is this the case? Many organizations have the impression that expressing these responsibilities by having the board sign something is either insulting or unnecessary.

There is something genuine and fundamental and brings that element of authenticity when you are asked to sign a document signifying and establishing an agreement or covenant between and among the board and the organization. Boards that insist on having a Covenant Agreement stipulating responsibilities are more likely to have supportive, engaged, and vibrant boards focusing on their work as opposed to being distracted by issues that do not relate to their core responsibilities.

What is included in the Covenant Agreement document? This document addresses a range of issues that each and every trustee must agree to. Topics include:

- Understanding the organization

- Financial support and philanthropic priority

- Involvement and support for fundraising activities

- Commitment to work

- Respect for the work and authority of the board

- Personal agendas

- Conflict of interest

- Confidentiality

- Adherence to The Governance Promise

For a sample of a Covenant Agreement, see Appendix G.

The Grass Is Always Greener?

The week had been a good one—productive, informative, encouraging, and affirming. All of the hard work covering the last few weeks and months had been rewarded by a fantastic visit by the accrediting team. The strategic plan, which had been the basis on which the accrediting team made its recommendations, was a carefully thought out document that articulated a compelling vision for the next five years with a nod to even longer term goals. This was noted in their report in which a verbal summary was given on their last day on site at the organization.

Scott Sullivan was completing his third year as head of school. The school, a kindergarten through eighth grade program, was connected to a large church in the community. Both the school and church were well established and highly regarded. While the relationship between the two was not perfect, the overall communication was adequate and the relationship stable.

Scott's first two years had been incredibly happy and productive. The relationship he had with his board, and particularly the board chair, Brian Gregory, had been exceptional. It was this board chair who was primarily responsible for Scott's selection and election by the full board. But after two years as chair it was time for Brian to step down. In his place, Terry Matthews was appointed. The third year was filled with challenges in that relationship. They simply did not see eye to eye. Nothing Scott could do was good enough.

This transition, from Brian to Terry, had not been a smooth one. Unfortunately the school's bylaws did not speak to whom the successor should be. Sometimes it was the vice chair and other times not. Of course, Scott had been caught in the middle of this and found himself in a position of not wanting to appear to be taking sides.

Following the departure of the accrediting team Terry asked to meet with Scott and informed him that she would be joined by the executive committee. Scott assumed that the topic would a "post mortem" on how the accreditation visit had gone and what the next steps would be. Scott hoped the meeting would be short as the next morning would be 8th grade graduation. When he arrived he immediately noticed six serious faces staring back at him.

Terry got right to the point and informed Scott that she and the executive committee were not pleased with Scott's work and were asking for his resignation! Scott was stunned. He could not believe what he had just heard. In the jumble of emotions he thought about his family who had moved halfway across the country for him to take what appeared to be a very attractive position. After he partially collected himself he asked, why? Very little explanation was given other than he and the board were not on the same page and that some of the staff thought him to be too demanding. There was no documentation, no warning, and no effort to try and resolve differences.

Scott thought, *Couldn't you have waited until after graduation?* He then asked what was to happen regarding the next day's commencement. He assumed they would not want him to participate. Then came the next shock—yes, they did want him to preside at graduation but that would be his last day! Scott started to refuse thinking this was outrageous. But instead he indicated that he would participate because he did not want the special occasion to be tainted by his resignation.

This story has a "happy" ending. A few weeks after this debacle another head at a K–12 school found out how poorly Scott had been treated and had an opening as the head of the lower school. Scott very gratefully accepted this position, allowing him and his family to remain in the community.

The underlying cause of this nightmare was a chair who was unwilling to set aside a personal agenda and look carefully at what was best for the school. Schools undergoing the transition from one chair to the next sometimes have the unfortunate experience of going from head (CEO) to the next believing the grass is always greener, and possessing the mentality that we can always find someone better. Terry thought she could find someone better. What she was probably seeking was someone who would agree with her agenda.

QUESTIONS FOR DISCUSSION

1. *What is your greatest concern with this story?*

2. *What does this say about the stability of the board?*

3. *What can organizations do to better prepare for the transition from one chair to the next?*

4. *Why do some boards believe that they can take this type of drastic action with no documentation, no warning, and no recourse?*

5. *Had you been Scott, what could you have done to build a relationship with Terry?*

6. *What could Brian and Terry have done differently?*

7. *Why can't we put aside personal differences and focus on what is best for the organization?*

8. *Could different language in the bylaws been helpful?*

Chapter Fourteen

THE ROLE OF THE EXECUTIVE DIRECTOR (CEO)

The executive director, or CEO, of the organization has a complex job with many moving parts. It is a position of enormous responsibility and filled with challenges, opportunities, great joy, and much frustration. Being the CEO means that "the buck stops here" and that the burdens and joys of leadership fall on this person.

Among the many character traits that best serve someone in this role is the ability to possess a level of self-awareness that sustains you when in the midst of many situations and difficult circumstances. Do you understand your strengths and weaknesses? Have you participated in the various psychological inventories that determine the kind of leader you are likely to be? Are these characteristics ones that will serve you well as a CEO? Are there aspects of your behavior that may benefit from professional development opportunities or coaching? Do you know the type of leader you are and want to become? These factors, and many others, are part of your self-awareness inventory that will prepare you for the challenges of leadership, management, and administrative work you face as a CEO.

One of the most challenging responsibilities of the CEO is working directly with the governing board and board chair. For the new or first-time CEO it may well mean working with an unfamiliar but important constituency. Even if the CEO is also a board member at another school or nonprofit organization, this is unchartered waters for most everyone who becomes a CEO. It is likely that most first-time CEOs have participated in few, if any, professional development opportunities that have focused on working with governing boards.

Many questions arise:

- Do you understand the dynamics of this relationship?

- Are you prepared to now report to a group of volunteers?

- Are you prepared to be evaluated by the board?

- Do you have any experience in working with/reporting to a volunteer board?

- Who can advise you about this relationship?

- Do your professional associations and organizations provide professional development opportunities?

- How well do you know the board chair and do you realize the importance of your professional relationship with this person?

These and other questions are just the beginning of what it is like to be a CEO in a nonprofit organization. Where do you begin and what are your priorities when it comes to this relationship? In your first ninety days the following should be your priority as you begin to build a relationship with the board of trustees:

1. Get to know the board chair and establish a relationship.

This relationship should be built on the seven most important characteristics needed:

1. Collaboration and Communication

2. Respect

3. Trust

4. Support

5. Attitude

6. Shared Vision

7. Leadership

Establish a specific time to meet one-on-one. You should consider once a week or every two weeks to sit down and discuss important issues impacting the organization. A breakfast or lunch may be just the right setting to establish this relationship. Somewhere away from the campus or location other than the organization as this will allow for fewer interruptions and more candid dialogue. This ongoing dialogue may include big ideas and small ones. It should include strategy and tactics as well as any issue that the chair may need a "heads-up" about. While day-to-day issues are not a priority, trustees and board chairs do not look too kindly on big surprises. Keep the chair informed about your activities and priorities and what you see ahead as opportunities and challenges.

2. Begin to build a relationship with each trustee.

Seeing and even working with Board members at board and committee meetings is only a part of getting to know the individuals on your Board.

These are effective tactics you can employ to do this:

- Meet with each individual trustee. Make an appointment at a location most convenient with the trustee and spend one-on-one time. Discover their interests—vocation, family, likes and dislikes, leisure activities, and anything that demonstrates your genuine interest in who they are. While this may be an opportunity for them to get to know you, the real matter at hand is to make sure they know that you are interested in getting to know them.

- Seek out board members at events. Almost every school and nonprofit organization has events throughout the year. This is an ideal opportunity to look for trustees and engage them in a brief conversation—including the opportunity to thank them for attending the event.

3. Develop networking opportunities.

Look for ways to build relationships with other nonprofit CEOs. Conferences, workshops, and meetings at the local, regional, and national level are all excellent ways to foster these connections.

The ability to communicate with someone you have gotten to know regarding a particular issue is an enormously important way to expand your knowledge of that issue.

4. Participate in professional development.

Seek learning opportunities that are directed toward both the CEO and board chair.

Being with other CEO/board chair teams is a unique way to share ideas and discuss challenges and ways to enhance and deepen this relationship. Participating in such opportunities together, the CEO will better understand the board chair's role and it will certainly enlighten the board chair as to the CEO's responsibilities.

5. Have a "Trustee Recognition Day" at your organization.

This can take a variety of forms, but setting aside one day a year to encourage staff, volunteers, and other constituencies to express appreciation to the board for their volunteer service and leadership is a reminder as to why they are on the board and will perhaps inspire them to stay focused on their roles and responsibilities as trustees. It is also important for trustees to find occasions to thank the staff and volunteers.

- - -

Serving as a nonprofit CEO or head of school reminds me of Jim Rohn's well-known quote concerning leadership:

The challenge of leadership is to be strong, but not rude; be kind, but not weak; be bold, but not bully; be thoughtful, but not lazy; be humble, but not timid; be proud, but not arrogant; have humor, but without folly.

Organizations and schools need great leaders and inspired boards! The impact that these organizations have requires nothing less than our very best. The days ahead must be even better than the days behind!

CASE STUDY #11

Changing Course in Midstream

The retreat had gone well—which was somewhat of a surprise. The small college's board of trustees could be difficult to work with and even more difficult to understand. So much was going well and the strategic direction had resulted in some amazing gains—enrollment, fundraising, student profile, faculty morale, and more. While everyone connected with the school should be feeling very good, there were a handful of trustees whose agenda did not recognize that the president's leadership and performance was not only satisfactory, but also outstanding.

Toward the end of the retreat the discussion turned to the accounts receivable issue. Accounts receivable is a challenge at many schools for a variety of reasons. However, every school recognizes the importance of having as small a balance accounts receivable as possible. Barton College was no different. The liberal arts college was well respected with a student population of approximately 1,400. Enrollment was stable but growing, and this had not always been the case. The new president and his team had done much to re-energize the college, and morale was very high other than within the board.

The question at the retreat then came, "What is our current balance in accounts receivable?" The vice president for business cleared her throat and proclaimed, "We recognize this has been something of a troubling issue but we are addressing it and we have seen some very positive gains in the last few months." As these words were coming out of her mouth a hand shot up and a new trustee, who was a former college president, stated, "I think anything that is not very close to a zero balance is unacceptable. During my time as a college president we rarely had this as an issue. What I am hearing about Barton is a huge concern." And there it was—his comments were momentarily met with stunned silence. But within a few seconds the other trustees erupted at the vice president for business insisting that more should be done—and done immediately. The mood changed completely and quickly the board became hostile, combative, and frustrated by what they were hearing. The former college president had altered the atmosphere in the room without understanding the back-story of why the college had adopted the earlier strategy.

What the current board of trustees nor the former college president knew was that years earlier the board had used receivables as an enrollment management strategy—a way to provide certain families with the ability to fund their children's education. In a sense, Barton College was serving as a benevolent creditor. At the time, everyone in the college's leadership accepted this strategy as policy and knew the result would be a higher than normal accounts receivable balance. Although there were a few remaining trustees from that time still on the board, they said nothing to support the vice president for business—knowing full well they were "throwing her under the bus."

The new treasurer and chair of the finance committee expressed shock that the college was in this situation. He demanded a complete review and a plan to eliminate as quickly as possible the accounts receivable issue. One of his first acts, without the knowledge of Barton's president or vice president for business, was to contact the auditor to gain additional insight into the matter. Unfortunately this auditor had little knowledge of the strategic use of need-based financial aid as an enrollment management issue. He proclaimed that the college was out of control and the vice president for business and president should be held accountable for resolving this matter.

The next several months included many difficult meetings in which there was a lot of talking and very little listening.

QUESTIONS FOR DISCUSSION

1. *Why had the former college president made his statement without an understanding of the unique circumstances that led to the higher than normal accounts receivable balance?*

2. *Why did the board react in such a hostile manner?*

3. *What reasons can you give why the few trustees who knew about and had voted for the enrollment management strategy said nothing when the issue surfaced?*

4. *Why did the treasurer not inform the president or vice president for business about the conversation with the auditor?*

5. *Should the president and/or vice president for business have spoken up at the retreat to explain the earlier strategy?*

6. *What does this story say about the relationship between the board, the president, and the vice president for business?*

7. *How will this story play out?*

8. *What relationship issues need to be addressed for the outcome to be positive?*

Chapter Fifteen

THE ROLE
OF THE DIRECTOR
OF ADVANCEMENT
(CHIEF DEVELOPMENT
OFFICER)

It is universally agreed that the board of trustees has a direct role and responsibility to ensure the organization has the resources necessary to not only sustain the organization but position it in such a way that it thrives.

The director of advancement, or chief development officer, has a unique relationship with the governing board. Because both fundraising and the marketing of the organization are critical to its ability and opportunity to fulfill its mission, the person in this role works closely with the entire board.

The titles and responsibilities of this office vary widely among schools and nonprofit organizations. Development goes under numerous names including:

- Resource Development

- Advancement

- External Affairs

- External Relations

- Fundraising

The responsibilities vary as well. For some K–12 independent schools, development may include not only fundraising functions but also alumni affairs, communications, marketing, and admissions. Depending on the size and structure of the nonprofit organizations, they may lump development and fundraising along with marketing, communications, and any external relations functions—even though these activities and roles are quite unique—into a single office or even one individual.

For purposes of this chapter our focus is on the person who is the individual who holds the responsibility for reporting directly to the executive director (CEO, head of school, etc.). As the director of advancement, this individual works directly with the board of trustees in the following ways:

Serves as a liaison with the development committee of the board.

Working with the development committee of the board is near the top of the list of responsibilities for every director of development. This will include: in conjunction with the committee chair, working on the agenda, preparing all materials for the committee's review, leading or participating in all committee discussions, attending all board meetings, and providing the chair with the data and information needed to give the committee report.

It is also critical that the director of development have the best possible relationship with the committee's chair. Depending on the school or organization this chair may change every year or two years requiring the development officer to work with or "train" someone with somewhat limited fundraising experience. Continuity is an important factor in success. However, this may be difficult to achieve.

One of the most important aspects of this relationship is the ability to equip the committee chair with the most effective way to communicate to the board the necessity of its role in giving and participating in the organization's fundraising priorities. Establishing this as a priority will enable the board to set a more aggressive goal than 100 percent participation. Challenging the board in appropriate and meaningful ways will set the stage for more dynamic results.

Works with the executive director and development committee to formulate all aspects of the fundraising plan.

Fundraising plans typically fall under one of these categories:

- Major or capital gifts

- Annual fund

- Endowment and planned giving

- Special events

- Small capital or programmatic projects

The director of development, or advancement, has an important relationship with the board's development committee. The director and the development committee provide strategic direction for the organization's fundraising objectives. The development committee is also charged with formulating the plan and goal to raise money from the board of trustees. The director of development works with the committee to ensure that there is 100 percent participation from board.

The director of development, the executive director, and the development committee will collaborate to set the annual fund goal and possibly other fundraising goals. The annual fund is particularly important in that there will be a line in the budget that corresponds to some or all of the total of the annual fund goal.

It is likely that the director of development will find it necessary to provide the strategic direction to the development committee that enables this group to carry out the task of soliciting the board in a way that will maximize results.

Works with the executive director and strategic planning committee to provide fundraising information for the strategic initiatives that require additional funding.

In other words, connecting the strategic plan with the most useful mechanism to fund that portion of the plan. Often the strategic planning process does not effectively engage the development leadership in looking at existing funding opportunities and challenges that must be addressed as part of defining the strategic direction. Such an initiative without understanding revenue sources is not only inadequate but fails to uncover potential support.

Works with the executive director to create a plan that encourages all trustees to participate in professional development.

It's important to find learning opportunities for the board that are specifically related to its role in fundraising. This is also a place for the development committee chair to demonstrate leadership and "lead by example" by participating in professional development opportunities.

Develops the information utilized in the new trustee orientation program.

Along with the executive director and chair of the development committee, the director of advancement leads this portion of the orientation session.

Works with the committee on trustees by identifying prospective trustees.

While it may be rare for the chief development officer to be included on the committee on trustees, there is good reason to have this person, along with the CEO, as an ex-officio member of this committee. These two individuals in these two incredibly important staff roles are in key positions to provide unique insight about prospective trustees being considered.

Clearly fundraising has been established as one of the more important factors when considering someone for the board. If this is true, then it follows the board would want the best information possible. The argument against this might be that the development officer could simply pass along names to the CEO for committee discussion. However, questions could surface in the meeting that the CEO may not be in the best position in which to respond. It is the information and the input that is vital to the process.

- - -

What may be best for the school or organization is to position the chief development officer as the number two staff person. Both perception and reality are a part of this strategy. The board of trustees is going to recognize and realize that development, the fundraising and revenue-generating arm of the organization, is placed directly behind the CEO. The chief development officer will be viewed as a leader worthy of all that goes with being one of the most valued members of the staff.

The other central message has to do with sustainability. We live in challenging times in which there are many opportunities but also many threats to not just thriving, but surviving. Where the chief development officer is placed in the hierarchy says something special about the organization.

A Matter of Trust

It was just like clockwork. On the days the board's development committee met, the committee chair, Laura, always called the director of development, Tina, in the morning and the president, Tom, in the afternoon about an hour before the meeting began. One of the several interesting facets of these calls is that Laura never told Tina or Tom that she had called the other. What message was this sending about their relationship and what message was it sending about trust?

The organization had an excellent track record in fundraising. The number of donors and the number of new contributors was growing every year since Tina and Tom's arrival. They made an excellent team and the results were amazing. The two leaders were trying to work with the development committee but it was clear the committee had an agenda that questioned and second-guessed almost every decision. To the committee, the expectation was one of catch-up. The organization had experienced a poor decade in which very little was accomplished in raising money. It was as if the development committee wanted to make up the difference in two years—an unrealistic expectation that demonstrated the committee's lack of understanding of the fundraising process.

A Matter of Trust

Prior to each development committee meeting, Tina prepared the preliminary agenda, discussed it with Tom, and once they felt good about it, sent it to Laura for her input. More often than not, Laura would have little to say about the agenda. And then, the day of the meeting, the calls would begin. Laura would ask Tina more about fundraising "gossip" rather than a discussion regarding anything substantive. In addition she would ask Tina what Tom was doing—an indication that Laura thought he was probably not doing enough!

Then Laura would call Tom and ask the "how's everything going?" question—looking for any information that would suggest answers to "why aren't you doing more?" or "what are your impressions of Tina's performance?" Laura would never exactly phrase her questions or concerns in this way but that was clearly the underlying message—I'm questioning you, and as a trustee ("your boss") I have every right to do so.

Tina and Tom would compare notes and shake their heads about Laura. It was obviously important for this relationship to work—there was a lot at stake. However, neither Tina nor Tom knew how to move forward. They would ask:

- Why was she doing this?

- Did she not trust their work, dedication, and ability to get the job done?

- Was she purposefully trying to test what they each said about the other?

- Did she not believe they talked with one another?

- Where was the trust between board member and staff?

- What were Laura and the development committee looking for that wasn't being accomplished?

- Was there any evidence that suggested they were not meeting goals and expectations?

These were all troubling questions as the two staff leaders were not sensing the support and encouragement so necessary to gain the most out of this relationship.

QUESTIONS FOR DISCUSSION

1. *What does this story reveal about the importance of relationships?*

2. *Personalities and attitude play an important role in relationships. What can you glean from the personalities and attitudes of Laura, Tina, and Tom?*

3. *As the organization's CEO, what should Tom communicate to the board chair regarding the way in which the development committee was operating?*

4. *How could the board chair address what would be a delicate matter between two trustees?*

5. *Would it be appropriate to "confront" Laura and discuss the situation?*

6. *Should Tina and Tom simply wait until another committee chair is appointed?*

7. *Would Laura benefit and be willing to participate in a professional development opportunity (seminar or workshop)?*

8. *When trust is not obvious, how can that be reclaimed?*

9. *How would you resolve this matter?*

Epilogue

NONPROFIT ORGANIZATIONS ARE VITAL TO OUR FUTURE

"Never underestimate the passion and commitment of a small
group of dedicated individuals to change the world—indeed
it is the only thing that ever has."
—*Margaret Mead*

Nonprofit organizations are a vital part of our culture.
They have been a part of who we are as a nation from
the very beginning, and they directly impact every facet of our
lives: religion, health care, education, foundations, environment, literature, and the list goes on and on. There are about
1.5 million nonprofit organizations in the United States. And
the common denominator for every one of these organizations
is that they all are required to have a board of trustees or board
of directors. These boards are made up of women and men who

volunteer *their time, their talent,* and *their treasure*—an expression known to almost everyone who holds a leadership position in a nonprofit organization.

The passion and commitment of those who work in the nonprofit world is almost universal. These are individuals who desire to make a difference, to make a positive change in others, and to impact the lives of those they seek to influence. Why then do we allow a volunteer board of trustees the responsibility of developing the mission and vision of the organization? It is a complex question. But since this is the case and it is unlikely the government will change the requirement, we must make every effort to ensure that each organization has the very best volunteer board possible to carry out these responsibilities.

The opportunities and challenges of maintaining, sustaining, and enhancing these organizations is critical to the future of our society. We must be vigilant, and board and staff must work together to ensure that the days ahead are inspired and filled with opportunities to be a positive influence in this nation and around the world!

Through this book, I have attempted to convey how the governing board can transform the organization. Thoughtful, well-intentioned, engaged, and passionate leadership is required as this process unfolds to reveal the potential of the organization. A clear and compelling vision combined with this model for leadership—both board and staff—is the "game changer." My hope is that some of this will resonate with you and that your board will become and remain super!

Appendix A

SUGGESTED BYLAW TOPICS

The organization's bylaws are required to be a legal, nonprofit organization recognized by the IRS with the 501(c)(3) designation that allows for tax-deductible contributions. The form, length, and wording, vary from one organization to another. Below are the basic topics that most organizations should include in their bylaws.

1. Statement of purpose (the purpose, or mission, of the organization must be articulated in the opening statements of the organization's bylaws)

2. Power or responsibilities of trustees

3. Description of circumstances that constitute voting membership

4. Tenure of service

5. Frequency of meetings

6. Number and description of standing committees

7. Description and responsibilities of the executive committee

8. Election of officers

9. Power and responsibilities of officers

10. Terms of officers

11. Appointment of committee chairs

12. Tenure of committee

13. Statement of fiscal year

14. Dismissal from the board

15. Dissolution statement

REVISING THE ORGANIZATION'S BYLAWS

The process of revising the bylaws of a nonprofit organization can vary from one organization to another. It is critical that the organization's CEO and board chair be in agreement regarding the need for revision as well as what specific changes are being considered.

The process outlined below is one possible scenario that could be utilized:

1. The board chair and organization CEO agree on creating a bylaws committee with the specific charge of reviewing and revising the bylaws as may be needed.

2. This bylaws revision committee may include:
   - Three members of the board
   - The director of development
   - Board chair
   - CEO of organization

3. Determine which issues are to be addressed.

4. Consider having an objective perspective (consultant) to ensure that every issue is being considered. Having someone with experience and perspective could make a significant difference.

5. The consultant can incorporate revisions into the new draft of the bylaws.

6. Bylaws committee meets to work and make any necessary changes.

7. Changes are incorporated into a second draft for committee's consideration.

8. Final draft is prepared and sent to board.

9. Presentation is made to full board regarding revisions.

10. Board takes action on revised bylaws.

SAMPLE BYLAWS

Name of Organization
BYLAWS

ARTICLE I

Name

The organization shall be known as the [Name of Organization], hereinafter called the [Organization].

ARTICLE II

Mission and Purpose

The [Organization] is organized as a nonprofit, 501(c)(3) corporation, the mission of the [Organization] is to: Create programs and opportunities that inspire learning, advance knowledge, and build communities.

ARTICLE III

Board of Trustees

Section 1. Election. The [Organization] shall designate a board of trustees who shall by elected by a majority vote of the members of the board, which shall occur, except in the case of filling vacancies, at each annual meeting.

Section 2. Number. The total number of trustees shall not be less than eleven (11) members, nor more than twenty-seven (27) members.

Section 3. Term of Office. Each trustee will serve a term of three years. Members may be nominated and elected for one additional three-year term. Members may not be elected beyond the second term unless they have been off of the board for a minimum of one (1) year.

Section 4. General Powers. The board of trustees shall have the general power and authority to manage and conduct the affairs of the [Organization] and shall have full power, by majority vote, to adopt rules and regulations governing the action of the board of trustees.

ARTICLE IV
Meetings

Section 1. Regular Meetings. The board of trustees shall meet at least quarterly at a time and place designated by the board.

Section 2. Annual Meeting. One of the four regular meetings shall be designated as the Annual Meeting. The purpose being the election of officers and the transaction of other business of the [Organization].

Section 3. Special Meetings. Special meetings may be called by the chair of the board of trustees or a majority of the board. The person or persons authorized to call special meetings shall provide written or electronic notice of the time and location of the meeting and state the purpose thereof. No other matter shall be considered or discussed by the board of trustees at such special meeting except upon unanimous vote of the trustees present.

Section 4. Notice and Waiver. Notice of regular or special meetings of the board of trustees must be made in writing or in electronic form at least seven (7) days in advance of the meeting date. The attendance of a trustee at any meeting shall constitute a waiver of notice of such meeting.

Section 5. Quorum. A quorum shall consist of a majority of the trustees present at the meeting. If at any meeting less than a quorum is present, the majority may adjourn the meeting without further notice.

Section 6. Vacancy. Any vacancy occurring on the board of trustees shall be filled by a majority vote of the remaining trustees upon the recommendation of the committee on trustees. Each person so elected shall serve until the duration of the unexpired term. They shall be eligible for election for one full, three-year term.

Section 7. Resignation. A trustee may resign from the board of trustees at any time by giving notice of resignation in writing, or e-mail addressed to the chair of the board.

Section 8. Removal. Any trustee may be removed by a majority vote of the remaining trustees at any meeting of the board of trustees. Such action may be the result of failure to act in the best interests of the [Organization], failure to adhere to the principles described in the Covenant Agreement, or any other action which demonstrates a lack of support for the mission of the [Organization].

ARTICLE V

Officers

Section 1. Designation of Officers. The officers of the [Organization] shall be the chair, vice chair, secretary, and treasurer. The same person may hold no more than one office simultaneously.

Section 2. Election. The officers of the [Organization] shall be elected at the designated annual meeting by a majority of the vote of the members of the board of trustees. Each officer shall be elected for a term of two years. Officers may be elected for two additional two-year terms. No officer shall serve more than six consecutive years in the same office.

Section 3. Removal. Any officer may be removed by a majority vote of the board of trustees for failure to fulfill the duties as prescribed by these bylaws, conduct detrimental to the [Organization], or for any other purpose judged to be not in keeping with the best interests of the [Organization].

Section 4. Vacancy. A vacancy in any office for whatever reason may be filled by the board of trustees for the unexpired portion of the term.

Section 5. Chair. The chair of the board of trustees shall be the chief volunteer officer of the [Organization]. The chair will lead the board of trustees in performing its duties and responsibilities. These shall include; presiding at all meetings of the board, serving as an ex-officio of all board committees, drafting and updating as necessary the Covenant Agreement, working in partnership with the CEO, and performing other duties as may be required by these bylaws and the board of trustees.

Section 6. Vice Chair. In the absence of the chair, for whatever reason, the vice chair shall perform all duties of the chair of the board. When so acting, the vice chair shall have all powers, responsibilities, and limitations of the chair. The vice chair shall have such other powers and responsibilities and perform such other duties prescribed by the board of trustees and the chair. Upon completion of the chair's term of office, the vice chair shall accede to the office of chair.

Section 7. Secretary. The secretary shall keep the minutes of the meetings of the board of trustees; ensure that all notices are duly given in accordance with the provisions of these bylaws or as required by law; and perform other such duties as from time to time may be assigned by the chair or by the board of trustees.

Section 8. Treasurer. The treasurer shall be responsible for all funds of the [Organization]; receive and provide receipts for monies due and payable to the [Organization]; deposit all such monies in the name of the [Organization]; keep and maintain adequate and correct accounts; and render reports and accountings to the trustees. The treasurer shall also be the chair of the finance committee. The treasurer shall perform all duties incident to the office of treasurer and any other duties that may be required by these bylaws or prescribed by the board of trustees.

ARTICLE VI

Executive Committee

Section 1. The executive committee of the board of trustees shall consist of the officers of the board, the chairs of the standing committees, and two (2) additional members of the board. The officers of the board shall be responsible for appointing these two members.

Section 2. The chair of the board of trustees shall serve as the chair of the executive committee.

Section 3. The executive committee shall be delegated such powers and duties deemed advisable by the board of trustees, specifically including, but not limited to, the power to act on behalf of the board at such times when the board is not convened in regular or special meeting.

Section 4. The executive committee shall be responsible for setting the preliminary agenda for all board meetings.

Section 5. A majority of the executive committee shall constitute a quorum.

ARTICLE VII

Committees

Section 1. Purpose. The board of trustees may establish standing committees to assist in the performance of its duties.

Section 2. Standing Committee. In addition to the executive committee, the other standing committees of the board of trustees shall include: the committee on trustees, the finance committee, and the development and marketing committee.

Section 3. Committee on Trustees. The committee on trustees shall be responsible for identifying, recruiting, training, and evaluating prospective and active trustees, consistent with the needs of the [Organization]. The committee shall nominate trustees to serve as officers and members of the board. The committee shall also be responsible for the annual program of orientation of new board members and the ongoing education and evaluation of the board, including organizing and facilitating board retreats. The committee shall consist of no fewer than four (4) members of the board. The chair of the committee on trustees shall serve on the executive committee.

Section 4. **Development and Marketing Committee.** The development and marketing committee shall be responsible for ensuring that the [Organization] maximizes its potential through fundraising efforts. In addition, the committee is responsible for the [Organization] developing and maximizing a marketing strategy to ensure strategic potential is achieved. The chair of the development and marketing committee shall serve on the executive committee.

Section 5. **Finance Committee.** The finance committee shall be responsible for ensuring the financial sustainability of the [Organization]. The finance committee prepares the preliminary budget and provides ongoing oversight of the budget during the fiscal year. In addition, the committee is responsible for supervising investments and ensuring the completion of the annual audit. The chair of the finance committee shall be the treasurer of the board of trustees and serve on the executive committee.

ARTICLE VIII

Parliamentary Authority

The rules contained in *Robert's Rules of Order*, latest edition, shall govern all meetings where they are not in conflict with the bylaws or other state laws pertaining to 501(c)(3) organizations.

ARTICLE IX

Indemnification

Unless otherwise prohibited by law, the [Organization] shall indemnify any trustee or officer, any former trustee or officer, any person who may have served at its request as a trustee or officer of another corporation, whether for-profit or nonprofit, and may, by resolution of the board of trustees, indemnify any employee against any and all expenses and liabilities actually and necessarily incurred by him/her or imposed on him/her in connection with any claim, action, suit, or proceeding (whether actual or threatened, civil, criminal, administrative, or investigative, including appeals) to which s/he may be or is made a party by reason of being or having been such trustee, officer, or employee; subject to the limitation, however, that there shall be no indemnification in relation to matters as to which s/he shall be adjudged in such claim, action, suit, or proceeding to be guilty of a criminal offense or liable to the [Organization] for damages arising out of his/her own negligence or misconduct in the performance of a duty to the [Organization].

ARTICLE X

Amendments

The Bylaws may be altered, amended, or repealed and new Bylaws adopted by a majority vote of the board of trustees present at any meeting. At least fifteen (15) days written or e-mail notice must be given of intention to alter, amend, or repeal the Bylaws or to adopt new Bylaws at such meeting.

ARTICLE XI

Dissolution

Upon dissolution of the [Organization], the board of trustees shall, after paying or making provision for payment of all liabilities of the [Organization], including expenses related to the dissolution, dispose of the assets of the [Organization] exclusively for exempt purposes of the [Organization] or distributed to another

501(c)(3) organization as determined by the board of trustees. None of the assets will be distributed to any officer or trustee of the [Organization]. Any such asset will be done in a manner in keeping with the wishes of the state court having jurisdiction over the matter.

Appendix D

COMMITTEE JOB DESCRIPTIONS

Included here are examples of job descriptions for two different standing committees found on many nonprofit boards. While not necessarily required, many times such descriptions will be included in the organization's bylaws.

DEVELOPMENT COMMITTEE DESCRIPTION OF RESPONSIBILITIES

The development committee of the board:

1. Coordinates the fundraising activities of the organization.
2. Advises the board on the financial goals through the annual fund campaign, through the budget, and on any capital or endowment campaign.
3. Supports the work of the development staff.
4. Encourages *all* board members to be involved in development activities.
5. Meets regularly to discuss issues and ideas that enhance the program.

While the development committee has direct responsibility for the organization's fundraising program, all board members must be informed and engaged in supporting the work of the committee as well as the development staff.

STRATEGIC PLANNING COMMITTEE DESCRIPTION OF RESPONSIBILITIES

Working with the executive director/CEO, this committee coordinates the creation of the strategic plan, including mission, vision, goals, and objectives, with the support and approval of the board. The committee is responsible for monitoring the plan once it has been approved and adopted by the full board. As progress for achieving the goals of the plan may fall to different board committees, the strategic planning committee works closely with other board committees to ensure objectives are achieved. The development of action plans is the responsibility of the CEO and the organization's staff unless the goal is a governance issue. The committee may include non-board members to address specific issues.

BOARD ORIENTATION SAMPLE AGENDA

The board orientation session is critical to setting the expectations for each new board member. Coordination of the orientation is primarily the responsibility of the committee on trustees along with the board chair and CEO. Attendance is also required of all officers and standing committee chairs. Everyone on the board should be invited to attend. Here is a sample agenda for an orientation session.

TOPIC	PRESENTER
Welcome by CEO and board chair	CEO & board chair
Introduction of each new board member	Board chair
Brief history of organization	CEO
Review materials included in board notebook*	Board chair & chair, committee on trustees
Review committee responsibilities	Individual Committee chairs
Review financial position	Treasurer
Discussion and signing The Covenant Agreement	Board chair; chair, committee on trustees; CEO
Q & A	Everyone

*Notebook will include; Bylaws, Committee Descriptions, Minutes, Listing of All Trustees, Listing of Key Staff, information related to the organization, and any other information needed by the board.

Appendix F

BOARD RETREAT
SAMPLE AGENDA

Under the guidance and leadership of the committee on trustees, the board chair, and the organization's CEO, the board retreat is a significant opportunity to set the tone of understanding issues and challenges, recognition of expectations, and ensuring the adherence of best practices to secure a bright future. Often, the board will have completed a self-assessment questionnaire covering a range of topics.

The retreat may have different priorities and objectives—strategic planning, preparation for a campaign, or the introduction of some change being considered.

Here are the topics likely to be included:

- Introduction to the retreat and overview of the agenda
- Review self-assessment questionnaire
- Review planning process
- Discussion and review of the mission statement
- Discussion of opportunities and challenges (SWOT analysis)

- Planning components and critical issues prioritized
- Distinction made between short-term and long-range strategic goals
- Action plan and next steps determined
- Summary of plan and adjournment

Appendix G

THE COVENANT AGREEMENT SAMPLE

The strength of the organization directly depends upon the willingness of the board of trustees to accept and carry out their leadership responsibilities for ensuring that the mission and vision of the organization is faithfully fulfilled. At the same time, the organization has certain responsibilities to assist and support the board in its work. This Covenant Agreement is the document that sets forth these conditions as stated below.

Board of Trustees:
1. *I accept responsibility*, that as a member of the board of trustees, I have certain duties I must perform for the organization to effectively and successfully function.
2. *I accept responsibility* for the future of the organization. As a member of the board I pledge to understand and support the mission and vision of the organization.
3. *I accept responsibility* to be knowledgeable of the organization's bylaws.
4. *I accept responsibility* for securing understanding and acceptance of the organization.
5. *I accept responsibility* to be knowledgeable of the organization's operations, programs, and policies. I will be objective in my evaluation of the organization.

6. *I accept responsibility* that while a member of this board I will make it a philanthropic priority for my giving.

7. *I accept responsibility* to make financial contributions to the best of my ability. As a member of the board I will do all I can to ensure its financial well-being.

8. *I accept responsibility* to actively engage in fundraising activities on behalf of the organization. This may include soliciting individuals, corporations, and foundations. It may also include assisting in special events, acknowledging the support of contributors, and engaging in other fundraising activities necessary to advance the organization.

9. *I accept responsibility* for the time commitment necessary to carry out the work of the board and the organization. I understand this will include attendance and participation at board and committee meetings.

10. *I accept responsibility* in discharging specific duties that are assigned to me whether as a member of a committee or as a part of the general work of the board.

11. *I accept responsibility* to respect the work and authority of the board. I will be supportive of the decisions made by the board. If I am unable to accept the decision of the board I understand this may mean being removed from the board.

12. *I accept responsibility* for understanding and embracing the belief that conflicts of interest are unethical, inappropriate, and undermine the work of the board and the future of the organization.

13. *I accept responsibility* for respecting all opinions and discussions. I will not come to the board with a personal agenda nor will I impose my will to the detriment of the organization.

14. *I accept responsibility* to abide by the principles articulated in The Governance Promise.

For The Covenant Agreement to be effective and meaningful, the organization accepts responsibility to support the work of the board in the following ways.

Organization:
1. The organization will provide to the board all documents and reports necessary for the board to function efficiently and effectively.
2. The organization will make available any staff member necessary to discuss issues the board deems relevant and appropriate to its work. This may include staff and trustees working together on board committees.
3. The organization will make every effort to be responsive to any questions that the board believes is necessary to carry out its responsibilities to the organization.
4. The organization will, along with the board of trustees, abide by the principles in the Governance Promise.

Signed:

Member of the Board of Trustees	Date

Board Chair	Date

CEO of organization	Date

NOTE: While this document is not legally binding, it is essential that the board and the organization recognize that these statements should guide and inform their work together.

Appendix H

EIGHT REASONS
WHY BOARDS STRUGGLE

Nonprofit boards will, on occasion, begin to lose focus and direction. Addressing the eight issues described here will return the board to what is most helpful and productive.

1. Ineffective or poor leadership
As almost every organization knows, everything rises and falls on the effectiveness of the leadership. A weak and uninspiring board chair or member will greatly diminish the board's ability to carry out its responsibilities. The board and organization will suffer if recognizable and dynamic leadership is not present.

2. Deficiency in the selection process
It is imperative that the board's committee on trustees perform its primary job of identifying, recruiting, securing, orienting, and educating the individuals most in a position to make a positive difference to the board.

3. Lack of commitment and understanding of roles and responsibilities
This issue, of course, is directly related to number two above. If the board individually or collectively does not embrace its role, it is the responsibility of the committee on trustees as well as the board's leadership (officers) to turn the board in the direction of what its role is.

4. Insufficient or the absence of ongoing board education
Professional development opportunities must be available to trustees. Annual retreats as well as other occasions to educate the board will lead to a more engaged and committed board and one that accepts its responsibilities.

5. Failure to utilize the skills and talents that exist within the board
It must be communicated to every board member not only how they can collectively support the organization, but also the specific skills, experiences, and knowledge they possess that makes them an asset to this board. In the absence of this, board members may believe they are being underutilized and their contributions are not understood or appreciated.

6. Failure to communicate with and within the board
Every leader understands the value and importance of communication. When it is lacking, there is a tendency to substitute what may or may not be accurate information. The ability to continually craft the message for the board to manage its work and provide the best possible governance is critical.

7. Absence of a strategic vision for the organization
Lack of vision is a killer for the organization and signals to the constituencies that there is not much going on. Articulating a compelling vision is the joint responsibility of the board and the organization's leadership. It is a vital step to sustainability.

8. Failure to work in support or partnership with the organization's CEO
One of the most important components of an organization is the relationship between the governing board and the CEO, including senior staff leadership. This partnership is without question the difference between excellence and success or mediocrity and failure.

EVALUATING THE BOARD: KEY QUESTIONS TO HELP BOARDS SUSTAIN EXCELLENCE

As mentioned in chapter 11, the following areas of self-evaluation will help you create the framework to provide the data and information necessary for a board to sustain excellence. Take time now to work through this exercise.

PLANNING

The board should, almost above any other factor, be a group that devotes significant time to planning. The central questions in this area should include:

1. Is there a clear, succinct mission statement that is not only current but also understood by all trustees?
   ☐ YES
   ☐ NO
   What will it take to move to (or stay at) YES?

2. Is there a strategic plan and is there a process in place for periodic review of the plan?

☐ YES

☐ NO

What will it take to move to (or stay at) YES?

_____

_____

_____

_____

3. Have all facets of the organization been considered when formulating the plan?

☐ YES

☐ NO

What will it take to move to (or stay at) YES?

_____

_____

_____

_____

4. Do "action items" include a funding mechanism? Is there a way to fund the vision?

☐ YES

☐ NO

What will it take to move to (or stay at) YES?

_____

_____

_____

_____

5. Does the board establish annual goals for itself?
   □ YES
   □ NO
   What will it take to move to (or stay at) YES?

   _____

   _____

   _____

   _____

6. Do board members participate in professional development opportunities?
   □ YES
   □ NO
   What will it take to move to (or stay at) YES?

   _____

   _____

   _____

   _____

SELECTION AND COMPOSITION

There is nothing more critical to the success of an organization than the processes in place for the selection and composition of the board. Answer these key questions, elaborating as much as possible:

1. What is the structure of the committee on trustees?

   _____

   _____

   _____

   _____

2. Is the committee active and engaged with all board
   members?
   ☐ YES
   ☐ NO
   What will it take to move to (or stay at) YES?

   _____

   _____

   _____

   _____

3. Does the committee have a matrix of prospective board
   members that identifies skills needed—both short-term
   and long-term?
   ☐ YES
   ☐ NO
   What will it take to move to (or stay at) YES?

   _____

   _____

   _____

   _____

4. Is the size of the board a positive or a negative?
   ☐ YES
   ☐ NO
   What will it take to move to (or stay at) YES?

   _____

   _____

   _____

   _____

   _____

5. Are all committees functioning and effective?
   □ YES
   □ NO
   What will it take to move to (or stay at) YES?

   _____

   _____

   _____

   _____

6. Are the CEO and board chair included as ex-officio members of the committee?
   □ YES
   □ NO
   What will it take to move to (or stay at) YES?

   _____

   _____

   _____

ORGANIZATION

How the board is organized reflects effectiveness in meeting the goals and objectives of the organization. The key questions include:

1. Are the bylaws clear, concise, up-to-date, and followed?
   □ YES
   □ NO
   What will it take to move to (or stay at) YES?

   _____

   _____

   _____

2. Is the committee structure of the board valuable in meet-
   ing the demands of the board and the needs of the
   organization?
   ☐ YES
   ☐ NO
   What will it take to move to (or stay at) YES?

   _____

   _____

   _____

3. Does the board seek ways to involve all constituencies of
   the organization?
   ☐ YES
   ☐ NO
   What will it take to move to (or stay at) YES?

   _____

   _____

   _____

4. Does the board recognize and act on the difference
   between their responsibilities and those of the organiza-
   tion's administration?
   ☐ YES
   ☐ NO
   What will it take to move to (or stay at) YES?

   _____

   _____

   _____

   _____

5. Overall, does the board understand its responsibilities?
   □ YES
   □ NO
   What will it take to move to (or stay at) YES?

   _____

   _____

   _____

   _____

   _____

6. Are there individual trustees who are not effective in their
   role?
   □ YES
   □ NO
   What will it take to move to (or stay at) YES?

   _____

   _____

   _____

   _____

   _____

7. Does the board review its work and is this process mean-
   ingful?
   □ YES
   □ NO
   What will it take to move to (or stay at) YES?

   _____

   _____

   _____

   _____

   _____

ORIENTATION AND TRAINING

Orientation as well as ongoing training and education will encourage trustees to focus on being the best they can be. The key questions in this category include:

1. Is there a formal orientation session for all new trustees?
   ☐ YES
   ☐ NO
   What will it take to move to (or stay at) YES?

   _____

   _____

   _____

   _____

2. Is there a board policy manual and does it include information useful to becoming familiar with the work of the board and the organization?
   ☐ YES
   ☐ NO
   What will it take to move to (or stay at) YES?

   _____

   _____

   _____

   _____

3. Does the policy manual include a clear definition of conflict of interest and how the board addresses this issue?
   ☐ YES
   ☐ NO
   What will it take to move to (or stay at) YES?

   _____

   _____

   _____

   _____

4. Is there a structured, formalized program for board education?
   □ YES
   □ NO
   What will it take to move to (or stay at) YES?

   _____

   _____

   _____

5. Is funding available for board members to attend/participate in professional development opportunities designed for the board?
   □ YES
   □ NO
   What will it take to move to (or stay at) YES?

   _____

   _____

   _____

6. Does the board conduct an annual or periodic retreat as a way to explore a range of issues beneficial to both the board and the organization?
   □ YES
   □ NO
   What will it take to move to (or stay at) YES?

MEETINGS

Meetings set the tone for a "board culture" that in many ways defines who they are, how they operate, and the impact they have. Don't take lightly these questions regarding frequency and length:

1. Is the current number of meetings per year about right?
   Are more needed and why? Are fewer needed and why?

   _____

   _____

   _____

   _____

   _____

2. Do board meetings typically last longer than two hours?
   ☐ YES
   ☐ NO
   Why is this length too long, too short, or just right?

   _____

   _____

   _____

   _____

   _____

3. Is the agenda properly prepared and reviewed by the officers or executive committee prior to the meeting?
   ☐ YES
   ☐ NO
   What will it take to move to (or stay at) YES?

   _____

   _____

   _____

   _____

   _____

4. Is the agenda and supporting documentation sent to board members prior to the board meeting?
   □ YES
   □ NO
   What will it take to move to (or stay at) YES?

   ----

5. Do committees meet at intervals between board meetings?
   □ YES
   □ NO
   What will it take to move to (or stay at) YES?

   ----

6. Is the staff liaison role understood and respected by board committees?
   □ YES
   □ NO
   What will it take to move to (or stay at) YES?

   ----

7. Are committee reports effective and useful?
   □ YES
   □ NO
   What will it take to move to (or stay at) YES?

8. Is financial information presented and conveyed in a manner that non-financial people can easily understand?
   □ YES
   □ NO
   What will it take to move to (or stay at) YES?

INDIVIDUAL TRUSTEES

Because each trustee is a key member of the board, the manner in which each trustee does their job is essential. The key questions for the specific trustee are:

1. Is the board member prepared for both committee and board meetings?
   □ YES
   □ NO
   What will it take to move to (or stay at) YES?

2. Does each member capably perform assigned as well as
   volunteered responsibilities?
   ☐ YES
   ☐ NO
   What will it take to move to (or stay at) YES?

   _____

   _____

   _____

   _____

3. Does the board member recommend others to serve on the
   board?
   ☐ YES
   ☐ NO
   What will it take to move to (or stay at) YES?

   _____

   _____

   _____

   _____

4. Does the board member give as generously as possible?
   ☐ YES
   ☐ NO
   What will it take to move to (or stay at) YES?

   _____

   _____

   _____

   _____

5. Does the board member recommend donors and solicit support?
   □ YES
   □ NO
   What will it take to move to (or stay at) YES?

6. Does the board member respect the work of the entire board?
   □ YES
   □ NO
   What will it take to move to (or stay at) YES?

7. Does the board member fully embrace and defend issues such as confidentiality and conflict of interest?
   □ YES
   □ NO
   What will it take to move to (or stay at) YES?

CEO/EXECUTIVE DIRECTOR

The relationship between the CEO, the board chair, and the entire governing board is critical to the health and sustainability of the organization. The key questions that support this relationship include:

1. Does the board support the CEO and view his or her role as one of partnership and collaboration?
   ☐ YES
   ☐ NO
   What will it take to move to (or stay at) YES?

   _____

   _____

   _____

   _____

   _____

2. Does the CEO establish annual goals and set goals that reflect the mission and vision of the organization?
   ☐ YES
   ☐ NO
   What will it take to move to (or stay at) YES?

   _____

   _____

   _____

   _____

   _____

3. Does the board have in place a fair and helpful way to evaluate the work of the CEO?
   □ YES
   □ NO
   What will it take to move to (or stay at) YES?

   _____

   _____

   _____

   _____

4. Is the evaluation presented in a way that demonstrates respect for the work performed by the CEO and the staff?
   □ YES
   □ NO
   What will it take to move to (or stay at) YES?

   _____

   _____

   _____

   _____

5. Does the board provide in the budget continuing education and professional development opportunities for the CEO?
   □ YES
   □ NO
   What will it take to move to (or stay at) YES?

   _____

   _____

   _____

   _____

THE TOP TEN BOARD DEVELOPMENT ISSUES THAT IMPACT YOUR ORGANIZATION

While there are many influences and influencers mentioned in *The Board Game*, there are ten I have singled out and identified as those that are the most powerful. Utilizing the well-known countdown format, we begin with . . .

#10—ATTITUDE IS EVERYTHING

*"Nothing can stop someone with the right mental attitude
from achieving their goal; nothing on earth can help someone
with the wrong mental attitude."*

—*Thomas Jefferson*

A positive attitude is essential. If you don't think so wait until you encounter someone with a really bad one and then try to work together to achieve certain goals. A person's outlook, or view of the world, has so much to do with how well they will relate to others. Do members of your board have a positive attitude? Are they team players with the kind of can-do attitude that inspires and encourages others? Do they value working together and recognize that consensus and team-building foster commitment to the organization as opposed to focusing on self-interest?

Whether a board member or nonprofit leader, attitude will define the organization in important ways and serves as a revealing expectation of what "being your best by doing your best" really means. Board members should be leaders and leaders are those who inspire and encourage, individuals who set an example of what is possible.

The key in having board members who exhibit a positive attitude is to *recruit* them. The committee on trustees is charged with identifying prospective trustees. I believe one of the most important characteristics that this committee should consider is attracting someone who possesses a positive attitude!

#9—FINDING BALANCE FROM THE BOARD

> "If we are together nothing is impossible,
> if we are divided all will fail."
> —*Sir Winston Churchill*

Both the board chair and all trustees must avoid whatever *extremes* they bring to the boardroom. Discovering common ground and ways of working together for the good of the organization adds both strength and sustainability. The value of teamwork is enormously important.

Every trustee comes to the board with strengths and weaknesses, likes and dislikes, and expertise and experiences. Much of this is valuable and certainly some of it is the reason that they were attractive as prospective board candidates in the first place. Having said that, board members may also arrive on the scene with strongly held opinions—perhaps too strongly held opinions. These opinions, whether professional or personal, can spill over into their board role and become unwarranted agendas. The agendas may replace what is best for the organization. In these situations trustees have gone too far trying to force others to consider personal perspectives as organizational priorities.

Let me provide an example where strengths taken too far become detrimental. In this scenario the person comes on the board because of a particular knowledge of all matters financial. They have extreme views regarding cost controls, curtailing expenses, and making cuts as a way to advance the organization. When these attitudes come into conflict with organizational priorities and different points of view held by a majority of the trustees, then the trustee must step back and accept that the board must speak with one voice.

Finding balance is the most effective way to govern. Trustees should monitor their behavior and when this does not seem to be working, the board chair must step in and provide the leadership and perspective to remind the board "team" that what is best for the organization is what is best.

#8—BOARD MEMBERS WITH AN AGENDA

"All cruel people describe themselves as paragons of frankness."
—*Tennessee Williams*

Even the best boards are subjected to chaos and often the reasons center around those members who have an agenda. These board members see the organization only through their eyes, unconcerned with whether or not their view might be harmful and a distraction from the strategic direction of the organization.

It never ceases to amaze me when an organization becomes completely sidetracked by someone on the board who wants to hijack not only board meetings but also the organization to fulfill their wishes and desires. And, what is more amazing is the number of organizations that succumb to this agenda time and again.

To be sure many individuals come to the board with certain beliefs, even passions, about what they consider to be most needed. This is a good thing! However, it becomes a bad thing when it is your overwhelming reason for being on the board—even when you recognize it is not a part of the strategic direction for the organization. But you don't care—you are both concerned about that! You are wealthy, powerful, and seldom told you are wrong, so you bully the other board members into your way of thinking.

Why does this happen and why does the board allow this to happen? Why is this someone we want on our board? More often than not the board knows this person and their M.O. Do they believe they can change them? Get them to give to areas that most need support? It is rare that a "board bully" will change their stripes. In the end they are a huge distraction for the board, for the CEO, and for the organization—consuming enormous amounts of time and energy dealing with what this trustee wants and must have!

What is the best way to have the kind of board members who will come to serve and act in the best interest of the organization? The answer can be found in the process of board recruitment and how the committee on trustees carries out their work. This requires an investment in time that far too many organizations don't wish to pursue. These organizations miss the point that there is a direct correlation between the time invested in recruitment and the quality of the board member attracted to the organization.

What should be the composition of the committee on trustees? The overall size of the board will help dictate this. But, ideally the committee on trustees should include three or four members of the board of trustees, the chair of the board, and the CEO (Executive Director or President) of the organization. Including the board chair and CEO is essential to the process and these two may, if they believe necessary, recommend a particular individual not serve as a trustee. This type of relationship with an extremely important committee requires communication, trust, respect, and genuine leadership.

Someone with an agenda and resources may, at first, seem to be harmless—even helpful. But in the long run this agenda is more likely to be a distraction and destructive to the organization.

#7—THE VALUE OF CONSENSUS AND TEAMWORK

"We have committed the Golden Rule to memory;
let us now commit it to life."
—*Edwin Markham*

The issue of how a board of trustees carries out its work is one that impacts the organization in significant ways. The principles of teamwork, trust, and partnership are central ones I raise in my forthcoming book *The Board Game*. Throughout the book there is ongoing discussion about the board doing a better job of working together. After further reflection on the issue, I developed this list of ten reasons why consensus and teamwork is a productive way in which to resolve issues. Working together in a positive and productive manner will help focus attention on the strategic work of the board. I share this list with you in the hope that it will generate healthy conversation among your board.

Ten Reasons to Embrace Consensus as the Way to Address and Resolve Board Issues

Many of the decisions made by trustees are made by consensus. Why is this the case and why is this the most effective way to lead and govern?

1. First, define what consensus is and is not. Consensus has to do with the general agreement on a particular issue. It should not imply that the agreement has been reached without discussion.
2. The value of consensus is that it amplifies the most important characteristics that define the CEO and Board relationship: communication and collaboration. Are we

working together for common goals and to ensure the viability of the organization?

3. Consensus builds support among board members. The opportunity to encourage open discussion on a particular topic has the effect of building enthusiasm and a more positive response.

4. Think advisory. While a board certainly has fiduciary responsibilities for the organization many discussions and decisions are more advisory in their nature and impact. Providing advice and counsel and reaching a decision by consensus may be more helpful than the need for a formal vote.

5. Consensus is another way to describe teamwork. When the board and CEO are "on the same page" there is a sense of shared vision and common purpose, a "pulling together" in a direction that is positive and productive.

6. Treating one another with respect will result in working together, and working together will result in building a stronger organization.

7. Working toward consensus may reflect compromise but does so in the best sense of the word.

8. It's not all about you. While individual board members believe they have a compelling agenda, the ability to listen to other perspectives demonstrates a willingness to believe other ideas may be just as valid as yours.

9. There is strength in the concept of servant leadership. Leading by serving suggests an organization that values putting the organization above self.

10. The Golden Rule is golden for reason. Our objective should be to treat (and work with) others, as we would like to be treated!

#6—THE BOARD LEADERSHIP TRANSITION

"Leadership and learning are indispensable to each other."
—*John F. Kennedy*

"Rough waters are truer tests of leadership.
In calm water every ship has a good captain."
—*Swedish proverb*

Anytime there is a transition in board leadership for a nonprofit organization, there is a risk that the leadership will not be as dynamic, not as effective as before. Of course there is the possibility that the incoming leadership will be stronger and even better than anticipated. Regardless, this transition from one board chair to the next may create some anxiety in the board and organization. Ideally, this transition should be a smooth, seamless one, and not necessarily noticeable to the organization's constituents.

One of the best ways to ensure the smooth transition in leadership is for this to be specifically included in the organization's bylaws. Is there a provision for the vice-chair to become the chair-elect? This is an important first step because it confirms that the vice-chair knows at the time that they are selected that the "grooming" has begun that eventually leads this person to become chair of the board. Prior to someone being identified as a future vice-chair (and, therefore, a future chair), the committee on trustees and the CEO should be completely involved in this discussion and selection. Their participation in this process is fundamentally important and a crucial factor in making the transition work.

The committee on trustees, the entire board of trustees, and the organization's CEO must collaborate and communicate to make certain that whoever is selected as the vice-chair/chair-elect bring to the position the balance to recognize the various contributions and schools of thought represented by the personalities found on the board. Compromise, consensus, and teamwork are key factors to making the transition harmonious.

#5—THE BOARD HAS ONE EMPLOYEE

> "A basic tenet of governance is that the board
> hires the CEO who in turn hires all other staff."
> —*Jonathan Schick (author of* The Nonprofit Secret)

Most everyone in the nonprofit world—staff, board, and volunteer—understands one of the basic truisms that ensure these organizations possess the structure to succeed. And this truism is that the board of trustees has only one employee and that person is the CEO (or whatever title is unique to that type of nonprofit). It follows then that every member of the organization's staff, including volunteers, in some way ultimately reports to the CEO.

Way more than anyone would care to imagine, board members do not grasp this fundamental principle. There are numerous reasons for this, including a lack of training and education, poor attitude, and simply a belief that some rules don't really apply to them. The result is that trustees will infuse themselves into the day-to-day operational issues that are specifically not their responsibility. Certain trustees are unable to distinguish between what is operational and what is strategic, planning, policy, and mission.

This becomes a complex problem where trustees don't comprehend that they are meddling and micro-managing. Tragically, this behavior will often lead to threats and bullying. In addition, trustees may also believe they have unfettered access to anyone and everyone in the organization believing that "because I am trustee, you must do as I say." If the organization finds itself with this kind of individual on their board it becomes the responsibility of the board's leadership—either the board chair or the executive committee—to directly address this matter with the trustee. Some who read this will shake their head and say, "We have no such trustee." Congratulations. However, it is a short trip from not having someone who fails to get it, to having exactly this scenario. Once again, it is in the recruitment of trustees where this issue can be raised relative to setting expectations.

Another reason this behavior exists can be found in various organizational constituencies who believe that the board should know everything going on in the organization. The reality is actually quite different. There are numerous personnel issues, for example, where it is not appropriate and in fact not legal for the trustees to know. Yet many ask the question, "As a member of the board, aren't you supposed to know everything going on?"

The most successful strategy to avoid this nightmarish behavior is to not tolerate it in the first place. This suggests that the responsibility for making sure this behavior does not occur falls to the committee on trustees and their role in making the effort to find the most "mission-appropriate" trustee possible. This is a person who understands, respects, and agrees to the information regarding being a board member that is shared. Perhaps the first issue that should be shared with prospective trustees is that the board of trustees has one employee.

#4—FUNDRAISING IS FUNDAMENTAL

"You make a living by what you get.
You make a life by what you give."
—*Sir Winston Churchill*

"In good times and bad,
we know that people give because you meet needs,
not because you have needs."
—*Kay Sprinkel Grace*

Much is required from those to whom much is given.
—*Luke 12:48*

What is universally true about nonprofit organizations is that they each require financial resources (revenue) to sustain their operation, provide capital for major projects, and a healthy endowment ensuring sustainability into an uncertain future. While there are no guarantees, what we are objectively clear about is that these components are needed for an organization to contribute something significant to our culture and society. If it is true that those closest to the organization are best suited to be its biggest supporters, then it stands to reason that the board of trustees, collectively and individually, is in the best position to provide this necessary financial support.

When a prospective trustee is recruited there are many issues that must be discussed, including the issue that fundraising is fundamental at a very personal level—meaning trustees must lead by example when it comes to giving! Board members potentially bring many needed attributes to their service on the board and chief among these is the responsibility to give as generously as is someone's ability to do so. The committee on trustees (when recruiting), and specifically, the board chair has the responsibility of candor. It may also fall to the board's development committee to make certain that 100 percent of the board contribute. Nothing less is acceptable. There can be no disguising the fact that giving generously and supporting this process is the responsibility of each trustee. It may not be *the* reason someone was asked to be on the board, but it is most certainly *a* reason someone was asked to join the board. Never lose sight of the fact that for the board of trustees, *fundraising is fundamental!*

#3—EVALUATION IS THE KEY TO UNDERSTANDING WHERE YOU HAVE BEEN AND WHERE YOU ARE HEADED

"The past is prologue."
—*From* The Tempest *by William Shakespeare*

Does past performance determine or influence future activities? Maybe. The question might be, do you want to improve because you have not achieved to your capability? For the board of trustees the issue is, can we be better and how do we make this happen? Part of that answer may be found in whether or not the board evaluates its own work with the objective being improvement of their performance—not the performance of the CEO! That is an altogether different issue.

The board has an almost stated responsibility to demonstrate their leadership by evaluating the CEO. Using specific agreed-upon criteria, the board measures the CEO's job execution and communicates strengths as well as areas of concern. To maximize their own work, the board should look inward to determine their strengths and areas of concern. Their objective should be to aspire to being a dynamic, thriving board always evolving to be the best possible.

There are three different ways in which to assess how well they adhere to these responsibilities. The first is whether or not they have adopted The Governance Promise (Chapter 12) as the way in which they govern their behavior, attitude, and their actions. The second assessment mechanism is adherence to The Covenant Agreement (Chapter 13)—a document they have signed stating that they will uphold very specific responsibilities and respect both the work of the board and the organization.

The third way in which the board can review its work is the evaluation instrument and questionnaire found in Chapter 11 and Appendix I. This resource breaks down board performance and responsibilities into seven different categories with questions in each category designed to pinpoint areas where the board is fulfilling its responsibilities, areas where they are not, and areas that require additional work.

The elements found in these three different but connected board resources will help measure meaningful value and are, in every way, a key to realizing a bright future. To get somewhere as opposed to anywhere, a strategy and a way to measure the results of that strategy are essential to realizing potential.

#2—THE BOARD CHAIR AND
THE HEAD/CEO MUST CONNECT

"The best leader is one who has sense enough to pick
good people to do what he wants done, and self-restraint enough
to keep from meddling with them while they do it."
—*Theodore Roosevelt*

"If your actions inspire others to dream more, learn more,
do more and become more, you are a leader."
—*John Quincy Adams*

Of all the issues that constitute a nonprofit organization the most important is the relationship between the CEO and the board chair and governing board. This connection, this partnership will determine the organization's success and vitality. If this relationship is working well then the organization can truly focus on mission and vision. If this relationship is not working then the focus becomes: What's wrong? How do we make it right? Where do we go to get the professional assistance we need?

To truly understand the underlying issues that bring clarity to this challenge, one must return to those seven fundamental characteristics that define what makes it work:

- *Collaboration and Communication:* Working together and regular, ongoing communication is foundational for the relationship to be the best possible.
- *Respect:* It is extremely difficult to work with and communicate with someone whom you do not respect or believe possesses the character and integrity that is an absolute requirement.
- *Trust:* If there is respect, trust soon follows. The ability to believe in what each other is sharing carries with it enormous importance.

- *Support:* What is all too often absent is a board chair who supports the head or CEO—especially when other board members are attempting to interfere with this leader's ability to manage the organization. Knowing you have the support of the board chair brings confidence to do what needs to be done.
- *Shared Vision:* When the board chair and head/CEO are "on the same page" with regard to the future of the organization, it suggests an organization that is thriving and meeting the needs articulated in the mission.
- *Attitude:* People who are positive, who see the world in an optimistic way, and who recognize they are blessed and in a position to share that outlook with others are in the best possible position to influence the organization in dynamic ways.
- *Leadership:* The ability and opportunity to encourage, to inspire, and to bring out the best in others is a character trait that is vital. Can you be at the same time strong, kind, bold, thoughtful, humble, proud, and have a sense of humor? Then you might just be a leader.

#1—PARTNERSHIP TRUMPS HIERARCHY EVERY TIME

"Never impose on others
what you would not choose for yourself."
— *Confucius*

"Teamwork is the ability to work together toward
a common vision. The ability to direct individual
accomplishment toward organizational objectives."
—*Andrew Carnegie*

Working together to achieve mission and vision trumps any other way to accomplish the same thing. Nonprofit organizations are essential to the very fabric of this country and too important to allow the intrusion of politics, personal agendas, poor attitudes, and other issues to hurt any organization. And yet this happens because human nature kicks in and we allow, are unaware of, or even encourage individuals who possess these less than stellar traits to be on our boards. Of course, none of these individuals would recognize any failure on their part to be the best trustee. Just ask any one of them!

In a 501(c)(3) organization, a governing board is required. They have the legal and fiduciary responsibility for sustaining the organization. They "hold in trust" the organization and, therefore, are at the top of the organizational chart. The CEO (executive director or president) reports to the board. This has worked well for years, and many organizations thrive in this environment.

But how do we get from good to great in this hierarchal reality? What is really at stake? Is working together more important, more valuable than working in a "who works for whom" mentality? The answers can be found in genuine partnership—genuine teamwork. It is a recognition that working together is the value-added benefit that is truly at the heart of servant leadership and what makes nonprofit organizations unique in our culture. It is this unique characteristic that acknowledges, *It's not all about me!* Is there a time and place for this hierarchy? Absolutely. There are certain circumstances that dictate a chain of command and a "buck stops here" approach.

The example of vision, or strategic planning, provides a peek into what genuine partnership can look like. Often several organizational constituencies are involved with the board, having ultimate responsibility for the direction of the organization. Why not include the CEO and senior staff in partnering with the board to determine the path ahead—by not just providing input but by acknowledging the special gifts each person brings to the enterprise. There are people with significant skills who contribute something profound to the conversation, but outcomes are diminished if those individuals are not included. Board members should embrace this.

Embedded in all of this is the almost lost art of listening and an attitude of gratitude! We are so often hung up on our position in the organization (or on the board) that we forget the best strategy may be to sit down, be quiet, and listen to other perspectives. It is a hard lesson for all of us. This is not to imply that your opinion doesn't matter—it does. However, we too often believe nothing is more important than what we know and what we convey. As a result, we continue to miss opportunities to express appreciation for good work, acknowledge effort that demonstrates passion, and show grace when mistakes are made.

Perhaps what we may well have forgotten is found in the Golden Rule. The quote from Confucius is an accurate statement that reflects the message contained in the Gold Rule. Treating someone with respect and trust is certainly the way we want to be treated. Serving, sharing, listening, and caring have everything to do with what this strong bond that is genuine and vital. The partnership of the board, the CEO, and staff all contribute significantly to organizational success. And in the end nothing trumps that!

ACKNOWLEDGMENTS

Writing this book, designed in some respects to be a companion book to *The Board Game*, and in other ways a stand-alone volume on the importance of putting the right kind of board in place, has been a collaborative experience where I have been blessed with the input of many individuals both directly in the nonprofit world as well as those just on the fringes of this unique world that fly under the banner of 501(c)(3) organizations.

As with *The Board Game*, my thanks begin with the help, support, and creative direction so skillfully provided by Kyle Olund of KLO Publishing and Dan Wright of Dan Wright Publishing Services. The combined wisdom of these two publishing giants is simply remarkable. Their efforts have made all the difference and I am enormously grateful for their support. In addition to Kyle and Dan, I wish to express my appreciation to Rebeca Seitz of Glass Road Media Management. As my publicist and friend, she has been central to the marketing of this book. I'm thankful for her wise counsel, excellent judgment, and ability to connect with what I am trying to accomplish.

At the very beginning I wanted to include several illustrations that would add a touch of humor to the content. I was fortunate to discover the creative talent of Michael Tillotson. He was a pleasure to work with and very quickly caught on to my quirky sense of humor. My thanks to Michael for the wonderful illustrations that are found throughout the book.

To everyone whom I have met and talked with over the past year, I thank you for your candor, insight, and willingness to share your wisdom regarding nonprofit governance, board development, and looking at what it takes to create and maintain a viable and vibrant board of trustees. You give me great hope for a brighter tomorrow. While I can't identify everyone, here a few who I would like to especially thank for their support, encouragement, advice, and counsel: Kim Drake, Denny Thompson, Barbara Johnston, Monica Watson, Pat Campbell, Hugh Harris, Rick Newberry, Patrick Schuermann, Dan Haile, Kasey Anderson, Grant Kennedy, and Todd Jones.

I would like to express my appreciation to everyone who was kind enough to take the time to write an endorsement for this book, and to Julian Bibb for writing the foreword. Your work inspires me and I am enormously grateful for your contribution to this book.

This book is dedicated to my wife Courtney. She has loved me and been by my side through good times and challenging ones. She is the love of my life and an inspiration for everything I do. The book is also dedicated to our children Courtney Leigh, Robert, and his wife, Lauren. This book is also dedicated to my late father, Charles R. Mott, Jr., and late brother, Michael I. Mott, Sr. Both inspired me and I am grateful for the many contributions they made to my life. They were, and always will be, my heroes. I am blessed beyond what anyone could ever hope for.

Meaningful quotes by the famous and not so famous always inspire me in numerous ways. One of my favorites is an anonymous one. It says, "I aspire to inspire before I expire." Ever since discovering this expression many years ago it has become my adopted philosophy and leadership style. It is critical to dynamic leadership that inspiring and encouraging others brings out their best and results in what is best for the organization. My hope is that this book inspires you to be your best by doing your best and that it will serve as a resource you read and benefit from time and again.

ABOUT THE AUTHOR

William R. Mott, Ph.D.

Consultant • Author • Speaker

William R. Mott, Ph.D., works with many schools, other nonprofit organizations, and associations with governance, fundraising, marketing, and leadership challenges.

Dr. Mott's focus is on governance, specifically the connection between nonprofit boards and the organizations' senior leadership. Working with boards to deepen their relationship with the whole organization is central to his efforts. His books, *Super Boards* and *The Board Game*, in conjunction with his blog and workshops, reflect this passion and concentration.

His leadership roles include serving as a university director of development, executive director of a historic museum house, president of a college and two independent schools, and eleven years as president of his own consulting firm.

Dr. Mott holds a Ph.D. in educational leadership from Vanderbilt University's Peabody College. His B.A. is from the University of Mississippi. He and his wife, Courtney, are the proud parents of Courtney Leigh, Robert, and his wife, Lauren.

HELP FOR YOUR GOVERNANCE CHALLENGES

The Strategic Role of Governance

Board Retreats • Consulting • Presentations

As Dr. Mott has identified in his book, *Super Boards* and *The Board Game*, the relationship between the CEO and the governing board is the single largest contributor to the success of the school or nonprofit organization. Their leadership will be the determining factor in the realization of the mission and vision.

As a result, Dr. Mott's work extends beyond the writing of these two books. It also includes working with schools and nonprofit organizations to achieve success. Specifically, Dr. Mott provides the services and support to be the change needed.

Using *Super Boards* and *The Board Game* as the backdrop to have meaningful conversations with school or organization's leaders, Dr. Mott will conduct a retreat to include the CEO (as well as key senior staff) and the governing board. While the retreat may have multiple objectives, the overriding objective is to address a range of issues that serve to strengthen the relationship between these two.

This retreat will produce the following outcomes:

1. Identifies and resolves key issues that can significantly enhance your organization.
2. Creates a roadmap that provides ways in which the leadership of the staff and board can work effectively and productively.

227

3. Reviews and revises bylaws and other documents to ensure organization mission and vision are reflected in the documents utilized.
4. Utilizes interactive exercises to establish areas of concern and areas of strength.
5. Provides action steps to ensure that the leadership recognizes warning signs and how to address each one.
6. Establishes the seven characteristics that bring about meaningful partnerships.
7. Encourages adoption and use of the six principles contained in *The Governance Promise.*
8. Encourages the utilization of *The Covenant Agreement* that establishes the working relationship between and among the board and staff.

In addition to the board retreat, Dr. Mott works with the schools and organizations in training new board members through a board orientation session or seminar. Dr. Mott also provides coaching in his work with school heads, CEOs along with governing board chairs, and others on the board.

Dr. Mott is available for presentations, workshops, and seminars for school and nonprofit organizations and associations. Speaking engagements may be customized to fit both the topic and time available.

If you want to learn more, contact Dr. Mott at:

Bill@WilliamRMottPhD.com
www.WilliamRMottPhD.com
2000 Mallory Lane
Ste. 130-214
Franklin, TN 37067

ENHANCE YOUR EXPERIENCE

Case Studies, Q & A, and Much More!

Are you interested in continuing your experience with *Super Boards*? Wouldn't it be great if Dr. Mott could work with you and your organization and go more in-depth with the Case Studies found throughout the book *and* discuss the questions found at the end of each of the studies? In addition, Dr. Mott will assist you and your organization regarding other questions and issues you have with governance and board development.

Here is how it works: Call, e-mail, or text Dr. Mott to set up a time once a week or once a month to talk. After you have established a time frame, just set up a conference call for one hour and Dr. Mott will visit by phone with the CEO, board chair, committee chair, or any board member to discuss whichever issues he can assist your organization. The frequency of your conversations with Dr. Mott will determine your fee.

This is an easy and straight forward way to benefit from Dr. Mott's more than twenty-five years of experience as a CEO, board member, consultant, author, and speaker. Contact Dr. Mott today and begin creating your own super board!